GAS STATION ANGEL

Ed Thomas

Published by Methuen
in association with
the Royal Court and Fiction Factory

First published in Great Britain in 1998
by Methuen
Random House, 20 Vauxhall Bridge Road, London SW1V 2SA
in association with the Royal Court Theatre, St Martin's Lane,
London WC2N 4BG

Random House Australia (Pty) Limited
20 Alfred Street, Milsons Point, Sydney, New South Wales 2061, Australia

Random House New Zealand Limited
18 Poland Road, Glenfield, Auckland 10, New Zealand

Random House South Africa (Pty) Limited
Endulini, 5A Jubilee Road, Parktown 2193, South Africa

Random House UK Limited Reg. No. 954009

A CIP catalogue record for this book is available from the British Library

Papers used by Random House UK Limited are natural, recyclable products
made from wood grown in sustainable forests. The manufacturing processes
conform to the environmental regulations of the country of origin.

ISBN 0 413 72740 8

Typeset by Deltatype Ltd, Birkenhead, Merseyside
Printed and bound in Great Britain by
Cox & Wyman Ltd, Reading, Berks

Caution

The Royal Court and Fiction Factory present

Gas Station Angel

by Ed Thomas

First performance at the Royal Court Theatre Upstairs, West Street, WC2
on 3 June 1998

First performed at the Newcastle Playhouse, Newcastle Upon Tyne
on 6 May 1998

Sponsored by Barclays New Stages – Staging the New

The Royal Court Theatre is financially assisted by the Royal Borough of Kensington and Chelsea. Recipient of a grant from the Theatre Restoration Fund & from the Foundation for Sport & the Arts. The Royal Court's Play Development Programme is funded by the A.S.K. Theater Projects. Supported by the National Lottery through the Arts Council of England. Royal Court Registered Charity number 231242.

Barclays New Stages – Staging the New continues a six-year partnership with the Royal Court, developed through the ground-breaking **Barclays New Stages** awards and festivals.

This new initiative promotes the exploration of innovation in form and staging, with four new productions and a stage design conference:

- **THE CHAIRS** by Eugène Ionesco, translated by Martin Crimp
  19 November - 31 January 1998

- **NEVER LAND** by Phyllis Nagy
  8 January - 7 February 1998

- **I AM YOURS** by Judith Thompson
  20 February - 21 March 1998

- **GAS STATION ANGEL** by Ed Thomas
  3 - 20 June 1998

  Ed Thomas won a 1995 Barclays New Stages Award for *Songs From a Forgotten City*

The conference will focus on modern theatre design and the needs of theatres in the new millennium.

Barclays New Stages – Staging the New is part of Barclays broad sponsorship of British theatre, touring high-quality productions through **Barclays Stage Partners** and celebrating excellence through the **Barclays Theatre Awards**. Theatre sponsorship is an integral part of Barclays overall community investment programme, which encompasses the arts, education and the environment as well as wide-ranging support for the voluntary sector.

Gas Station Angel

by Ed Thomas

Cast

Mati & Chambermaid	Donna Edwards
Marshall	Roger Evans
Gruff	Russell Gomer
Dyfrig, Keith & Mr Entertainment	Simon Gregor
Bri	Richard Harrington
Mary Annie	Valmai Jones
Ace	Richard Lynch
Bron	Siwan Morris
Manny	John Ogwen

Director	Ed Thomas
Design and Lighting	Peter Mumford
Composer / Musical Director	John Hardy
Sound Designer	Mike Beer
Producer	Mike Parker
Assistant Director	Steve Fisher
Assistant Design and Lighting	John Buswell
Production Manager	Ian Buchanan
Company Stage Manager	Maris Sharp
Deputy Stage Manager	Sandra Grieve
Costume Supervisor	Sam Mealing
Set Construction	Miraculous Engineering
Scenic Artist	Patrick Hamilton

The Royal Court and Fiction Factory would also like to thank the following with this production: Wardrobe care by Persil and Comfort courtesy of Lever Brothers Ltd, refrigerators by Electrolux and Philips Major Appliances Ltd; kettles for rehearsals by Morphy Richards; video for casting purposes by Hitachi; backstage coffee machine by West 9; furniture by Knoll International; freezer for backstage use supplied by Zanussi Ltd 'Now that's a good idea.' Hair styling by Carole at Moreno, 2 Holbein Place, Sloane Square 0171-730-0211; Closed circuit TV cameras and monitors by Mitsubishi UK Ltd. Natural spring water from Aqua Cool, 12 Waterside Way, London SW17 0XH, tel. 0181-947 5666. Overhead projector from W.H. Smith; Sanyo U.K for the backstage microwave; Watford Palace Theatre; Alison Sewell - student placement; Tesco's Superstore, Cardiff.

Ed Thomas (writer and director)

Ed is the artistic director, producer and writer of Fiction Factory Ltd (formerly known as Y Cwmni). He has worked extensively in theatre, television, film and radio, winning numerous awards - including BAFTA Arts Foundation, BBC Arts and Cel;tic Film Festival Awards.

As a writer and director for theatre.

For the Royal Court: Song From a Forgotten City (& Y Cwmni. Touring UK, Europe and Australia).

Other theatre includes: House of America (UK tour & Festival of Perth); Adar Heb Adenydd (Welsh tour & Edinburgh Festival); The Myth of Michael Roderick (UK tour); Flowers of the Dead Red Sea (Tramway, Glasgow; Chapter, Cardiff; and Waterman's, London); East From the Gantry (Tramway, Glasgow; Kiev, Ukraine; Sherman, Cardiff; UK & Ireland tour); Hiraeth / Strangers In Conversation (Oriel Gallery, Cardiff); Envy (Welsh tour); Double Indemnity (Theatr Clwyd - as director).

Television includes: Hunllef Yng Nghymru Fydd, A Silent Village / Pentre Mud, Fallen Sons, Mind to Kill / Yr Heliwr, Satellite City.

Films: House of America.

Publications: Frontline Intelligence - New Plays For the Nineties (Methuen); Three Plays - House of America, Flowers of the Dead Red Sea, East From the Gantry (Seren).

Mike Beer (sound designer and touring engineer)

For the Royal Court: Song From a Forgotten City (Y Cwmni).

Theatre includes: Tom Jones (Mid Wales Touring Company); Up'n'Under, The Merchant of Venice, Diaries of Adrian Mole. Dracula, The Snow Spider, Matilda (Sherman, Cardiff. In house desginer 1991-92).

Theatre production and engineering includes: Cinderella (Alpha Studio); Enter Achilles (DV8 Physical Theatre, North American tour); The New Adventures of Noddy and The Witches (Clarion Promotions, UK tour).

Donna Edwards

Theatre includes: Up on the Roof (Queen's, Hornchurch); Cwm Glo, Loose Ends (Sherman, Cardiff); Love's Labours Lost (Mappa Mundi Theatre Co.); The Devils, A Prayer For Wings (Theatr Clwyd Co.).

Television includes: Mortimer's Law, Tair Chwaer, Glan Hafren, A Mind to Kill, Streetlife, Judas and the Gimp, Friday On My Mind, Angry Earth / Llid Y Ddaear, Child of Love / Calcon Fach Yn Ddwy, Heaven On Earth, Dinas, The Life and Times of Lloyd George, Off to Philadelphia in the Morning.

Film includes: Rebecca's Daughters.

Roger Evans

Theatre: Crash (tour UK).

Telivsion includes: Crime Traveller, The Bill.

Film includes: Human Traffic.

Trained at the Gulidhall School of Music and Drama.

Russell Gomer

Theatre includes: The Town That Went Mad (Volcano); Up 'N'Under, The Merchant of Venice, Macbeth (Sherman, Cardiff); The Castle, Hamlet, The Tempest (Moving Being Theatre Co.); Cyrano de Bergerac (RSC); House of America, The Myth of Michael Roderick, Envy, Flowers of the Dead Red Sea, Song From a Forgotten City (Fiction Factory).

Television includes: Skip Day in Splott, A Relative Stranger, Insect Life, Mwy Na Phapur Newydd, Iechyd Da.

Film includes: Boy Soldier, Street Life, Journey's End.

Radio includes: The Citadel, Flowers of the Dead Red Sea, Live at the Sherman.

Simon Gregor

For the Royal Court: Weldon Rising (& Liverpool Playhouse), Inventing a New Colour (RNT Studio & Bristol Old Vic).

Other theatre includes: The Front Page (Donmar Warehouse); Beauty and the Beast (Young Vic); Full Moon (Theatr Clwyd & Young Vic); Woman in Mind (Windsor Theatre Royal); Damned For Despair, Three

Judgements in One (Gate); Good Person of Setzuan (RNT); Master Harold and the Boys (Contact, Manchester); Marat Sade, Wild Honey, Happy Haven (West Yorshire Playhouse); Privates On Parade (Octagon, Bolton); Catch 22 (Dukes, Lancaster); Marriage of Figaro (Theatr Clwyd); Mabingoi (Moving Being Theatre Co.).

Television includes: Men Behaving Badly, The Keep, Love On a Branch Line, Blag, Avarice, Drop the Dead Donkey, Queen of Clubs, The Bill, Kavanagh QC.

Film includes: Bodywork, Last Seduction II, The Island On Bird Street, Life of Socrates, A Casualty of War, Young Toscanini, Escape From Sobibor.

John Hardy (composer / musical director)
Original music for film includes: Hedd Wyn, Streetlife.

Documentary series: Visions of Snowdonia, Egypt Uncovered.

Orchestral scores include: The Life Story of David Lloyd George (accompanied the Cardiff premiere of the rediscovered 1918 film), Blue Letters From Tanganyika (BBC National Orchestra of Wales, St David's Hall, Cardiff).

Opera includes: Flowers (toured by Music Theatre Wales - based on *Flowers of the Dead Red Sea* by Ed Thomas); The Roswell Incident (toured England and Wales); Mis Bach Du / Black February (Welsh National Opera, Fishguard Community); De Profundis (commissioned by the choir of Westminster Abbey for their 1998 *Century of Martyrs* celebrations).

Scored for Radio: A Clockwork Orange (radio 4).

Richard Harrington
Theatre includes: House of America (tour, The Fiction Factory); Un Nos Ar Faes Peryddon (tour, Spectacle Theatre Co.); Nothing To Pay (Thin Language/Made in Wales tour); The Snow Queen (Sherman, Cardiff).

Telvision includes: Iechyd Da, Tiger Bay, Pobol Y Cwm, Mind to Kill, Y Fargen, Aeronaut, Streetlife, Oliver's Travels, Halen

Yn Y Gwaed, Gadael Lenin, Broken Glass, Judas and the Gimp, Dafydd, Cwm Hyfryd, Civvies, Gopath, Splat, 1996, District Nurse, Swigs.

Film includes: House of America, Rampage, The Proposition.

Radio includes: The Assassin, The Elizabethans, The Great Subterranean Adventure, A Civil War, Three O'Clock at Ponty, Y Streic, Baby Baby, Night Must Fall.

Valmai Jones
Theatre includes: Jelly Babies, Cociau Gwair A Styciau Yd, La Malade Imaginaire, Le Medecin Malgre Lui, Tua'r Terfyn, Oliver (Theatr Gwynedd); The Snow Queen (Sherman, Cardiff); The Changelings (Theatr Clwyd).

Television includes: Pengelli, The Green Dress, William Jones, Jini Me.

Radio includes: Into the Dark, Yr Aelod, Tra Bo Dau, The Two Executioners, Jones A Jones.

Theatr directed includes: Pelgoch (Theatr Gwynedd); Bobi A Sami, Ywraig, Rigor Mortis (Theatr Baracaws - Founder Member).

Richard Lynch
For the Royal Court: Patagonia (including tour).

Theatre includes: The Mysteries (RSC); Macbeth (Theatr Clwyd); Hamlet, A Midsummer Night's Dream (Moving Being Theatre Co.); Flowers of the Dead Sea, The Myth of Michael Roderick, House of America (Y Cwmni); Abigail's Party (?); Kasper, The Castle, Victory (Moving Being Theatre); Malvinas (?); The Flies (?); The Fall And Redemption of Man (?); Godspell (?); Romeo and Juliet (?); Penderyn (?).

Television includes: The Proposition, Branwen, The Healer, Lifeboat, Thicker Than Water, Christmas Stallion, Rebecca, Bowen at Bartner, Babylon By-Passed, District Nurse, Breaking Rank, Sticky Wickets, Mwy Na Phapur Newydd, Yr Arwerthwr.

Film includes: Darklands, Watermarks, Boy Soldier.

Siwan Morris

Theatre includes: Equis, Rape of the Fair Country, The Journey of Mary Kelly (Theatr Clwyd).

Graduated from the Manchester Metropolitan School of Theatre in 1997. This will be her London debut.

Peter Mumford (designer and lighting)

For the Royal Court : The Strip (lighting design).

Other lighting designs include - for theatre: Wallenstein, Ion, Camino Real, Goodnight Children Everywhere, Henry V (RSC); School For Wives, The Winter Guest (Almeida); Mirandolina (Lyric Hammersmith); Simon Boccanegra (Munich Staatsoper); Richard II, Volpone, Mother Courage, Stanley, The Invention of Love (RNT); A Doll's House (Playhouse & Broadway); Sabina (Bush); Experiment With Air Pump (Royal Exchange Manchester). For opera: Fearful Symmetries (Royal Ballet); Fidelio (Scottish Opera at Edinburgh Festival); Luisa Miller, Madame Butterlfy, Falstaff, Tannhauser (Opera North); Die Soldaten (English National Opera); The Man Who Strides the Wind (Almeida). For ballet: Carmina Burana, Edward II, Nutcracker Sweeties (Birmingham Royal Ballet); Mr Worldly Wise (Royal Ballet). For dance: The Glass Blew In.

Set & lighting design includes - for theatre: Foe (West Yorkshire Playhouse, London & European tour); Odysseus Thump, Touching Heaven (West Yorkshire Playhouse & Tokyo). For opera: Parsifal (Welsh National Opera); Modern Living, Fidelio (Opera North). For ballet: Two Part Invention (Royal Ballet).

As a director for television, includes: Strong Language, White Man Sleeps, Wyoming, Heaven Ablaze in His Breast, Dancehouse 1990, Five Dances By Martha, Cosi Fan Tutte, Swan Lake.

John Ogwen

Theatre includes: Y Twr (Cwmni Theatr Cymru); Un Nos Ola Leuad (his own adaptation for, Cwmni Theatr Cymru); The Caucasian Chalk Circle, The Cherry Orchard, Leni (Cwmni Theatr Gwynedd).

Television includes: Y Twr, Tywyll Heno (& writer), Minafon, Saer Doliau, Deryn, Cyw Haul, Dr Who, District Nurse, Tylluan Wen.

Radio includes: The Archers.

TOUR DATES:

6-8 May
Newcastle Playhouse
0191 232 2336

12-13 May
Royal Flemish Theatre
Brussels
00322 217 6937

15-16 May
Theatr Brycheiniog
Brecon
01874 611 622

19-23 May
Theatr Clwyd
Mold, Flintshire
01352 755 114

27-30 May
Sherman Theatre
Cardiff
01222 230451

3-27 June
The Royal Court
Theatre Upstairs
0171 565 5000

30 June - 3 July
Swansea Grand Theatre
01792 475715

Derwen is an award winner under the Pairing Scheme for its support of Fiction Factory. The Pairing Scheme is a Government Scheme Managed by ABSA.

Fiction Factory
Theatre

Fiction Factory (formerly known as Y Cwmni) has since 1989 staged eight productions written and directed by Ed Thomas and in the process achieved huge and instant recognition within Wales and a cult status outside it. Its work has become synonymous with the renaissance in innovative text for the stage combined with ensemble theatre making of a distinctive and unforgettable kind. Fiction Factory is one of only two professional companies in Britain devoted entirely to the work of an individual writer.

Fiction Factory have recently finished touring a brand new production of *House of America* - in the UK during the autumn of 1997 and ending in Perth, Australia in the spring of 1998. Ed Thomas's other plays for Fiction Factory have also toured the UK, Europe, North America and Australia and his work has been translated into many languages including French, German and Spanish.

Song From a Forgotten City
Photograph by Brian Tarr

House of America, Flowers of the Dead Red Sea, East From the Gantry have been published as a trilogy by Seren Books (1993) and by Methuen in, *Frontline Intelligence - New Plays For the Nineties* (translated into French, Catalan and German).

Song From a Forgotten City
Photograph by Brian Tarr

Productions to Date:

1997-98	*House of America*
1994-96	*Song From a Forgotten City*
1993	*Envy*
1993	*Hiraeth / Strangers in Conversation*
1992	*East From the Gantry*
1991	*Flowers of the Dead Red Sea*
1990	*The Myth of Michael Roderick*
1989	*Adar Heb Adenydd*
1988	*House of America*

House of America
Photograph by Brian Tarr

Film and Television

The creation of Fiction Factory Films in 1993 widened the company's output. Its first production, a 50 minute drama documentary *Silent Village* won the Spirit of the Festival award at the Celtic Film Festival, and both it and its brand new situation comedy *Satellite City* have been BAFTA award nominated. Current projects in development include *Gas Station Angel* as a 90-minute feature, *Rancid Aluminium*, also as a 90-minute feature, and a brand new comedy *What a Wonderful World*.

For **Fiction Factory**

Artistic Director
Edward Thomas
Producer
Mike Parker
Administrator
Julie Whyte
Production Co-ordinator
Alun Morgan
Production Manager
Ian Buchanan
Tour Manager
Steve Fisher

For further details on The Fiction Factory you can reach them in the the follwing ways:

The Fiction Factory
Chapter
Market Road
Cardiff
CF5 1QE

Telephone 01222 300320
Fax 01222 300321
E-mail:
FICTIONFACTORYLTD@btinternet.com
or visit the Fiction Factory Website:
http://www.btinternet.com/
~fictionfactoryltd/

Fiction Factory is an award winning theatre, film and television company.

JERWOOD
NEW PLAYWRIGHTS

The Royal Court is delighted that the relationship with the Jerwood Foundation, which began in 1993, continues in 1997-98 with a third series of Jerwood New Playwrights.

The Foundation's commitment to supporting new plays by new playwrights has contributed to some of the Court's most successful productions in recent years, including Sebastian Barry's *The Steward of Christendom*, Mark Ravenhill's *Shopping and F£££ing* and Ayub Khan-Din's *East is East*. This season the Jerwood New Playwrights series continues to support young theatre with six productions including Conor McPherson's *The Weir*, Meredith

Oakes' *Faith*, Rebecca Prichard's *Fair Game* and Sarah Kane's *Cleansed*.

The Jerwood Foundation is a private foundation dedicated to innovative cultural initiatives supporting young talent. In addition to sponsorships such as the Jerwood New Playwrights, the Foundation is embarking on a series of new, large-scale initiatives. Currently these include the Jerwood Space, a new arts centre in central London offering low-cost rehearsal and production facilities to young artistic talent; and the Jerwood Film Prize, a screenwriting competition in association with Warner Village Cinemas, The Daily Telegraph, Channel 5 and Working Title.

The Beauty Queen of Leenane
by Martin McDonagh (Photograph: Ivan Kyncl)

The Weir by Conor McPherson
(Photograph: Pau Ros)

East is East by Ayub Khan-Din
(Photograph: Robert Day)

Mojo by Jez Butterworth
(Photograph: Ivan Kyncl)

The English Stage Company at the Royal Court Theatre

The English Stage Company was formed to bring serious writing back to the stage. The first Artistic Director, George Devine, wanted to create a vital and popular theatre. He encouraged new writing that explored subjects drawn from contemporary life as well as pursuing European plays and forgotten classics. When John Osborne's **Look Back in Anger** was first produced in 1956, it forced British theatre into the modern age. In addition to plays by 'angry young men', the international repertoire included Bertolt Brecht, Eugène Ionesco, Jean-Paul Sartre, Marguerite Duras, Frank Wedekind and Samuel Beckett.

The ambition was to discover new work which was challenging, innovative and of the highest quality, underpinned by a contemporary style of presentation. Early Court writers included Arnold Wesker, John Arden, David Storey, Ann Jellicoe, N F Simpson and Edward Bond. They were followed by David Hare, Howard Brenton, Caryl Churchill, Timberlake Wertenbaker, Robert Holman and Jim Cartwright. Many of their plays are now modern classics.

Many established playwrights had their early plays produced in the Theatre Upstairs including Anne Devlin, Andrea Dunbar, Sarah Daniels, Jim Cartwright, Clare McIntyre, Winsome Pinnock, Martin Crimp and Phyllis Nagy. Since 1994 there has been a major season of plays by writers new to the Royal Court, many of them first plays, produced in association with the Royal National Theatre Studio with sponsorship cfrom the Jerwood Foundation. The writers include Joe Penhall, Nick Grosso, Judy Upton, Sarah Kane, Michael Wynne, Judith Johnson, James Stock, Simon Block and Mark Ravenhill. Since 1996 the Jerwood New Playwrights Series has supported new plays by Jez Butterworth, Martin McDonagh and Ayub Khan-Din (in the Theatre Downstairs), Mark Ravenhill, Tamantha Hammerschlag, Jess

Walters, Conor McPherson, Meredith Oakes and Rebecca Prichard (in the Theatre Upstairs).1997-98 sees the first Barclays New Stages - Staging the New Season, which continues a six year partnership with the Royal Court, developed through the ground-breaking Barclays New Stages Awards and Festivals. The season has so far included productions of **The Chairs**, **Never Land** and **I Am Yours**.

Theatre Upstairs productions regularly transfer to the Theatre Downstairs, as with Ariel Dorfman's **Death and the Maiden**, Sebastian Barry's **The Steward of Christendom** (a co-production with *Out of Joint),* Martin McDonagh's **The Beauty Queen Of Leenane** (a co-production with Druid Theatre Company), Ayub Khan-Din's **East is East** (a co-production with Tamasha Theatre Company) and Conor McPherson's **The Weir**. Some Theatre Upstairs productions transfer to the West End, such as Kevin Elyot's **My Night With Reg** and Mark Ravenhill's **Shopping and F£££ing** (a co-production with *Out of Joint).*

1992-1997 were record-breaking years at the box-office with capacity houses for **Death and the Maiden, Six Degrees of Separation, Oleanna, Hysteria, The Cavalcaders, The Kitchen, The Queen & I, The Libertine, Simpatico, Mojo, The Steward of Christendom, The Beauty Queen of Leenane, East is East** and **The Chairs.**

Death and the Maiden and **Six Degrees of Separation** won the Olivier Award for Best Play in 1992 and 1993 respectively. **Hysteria** won the 1994 Olivier Award for Best Comedy, and also the Writers' Guild Award for Best West End Play. **My Night with Reg** won the 1994 Writers' Guild Award for Best Fringe Play, the Evening Standard Award for Best Comedy, and the 1994 Olivier Award for Best Comedy. Sebastian Barry won the 1995 Writers' Guild Award for Best Fringe Play, the 1995

Critics' Circle Award and the 1997 Christopher Ewart-Biggs Literary Prize for **The Steward of Christendom**, and the 1995 Lloyds Private Banking Playwright of the Year Award. Jez Butterworth won the 1995 George Devine Award for Most Promising Playwright, the 1995 Writers' Guild New Writer of the Year, the Evening Standard Award for Most Promising Playwright and the 1995 Olivier Award for Best Comedy for **Mojo**. Phyllis Nagy won the 1995 Writers' Guild Award for Best Regional Play for **Disappeared**. Michael Wynne won the 1996 Meyer-Whitworth Award for **The Knocky**. Martin McDonagh won the 1996 George Devine Award, the1996 Writers' Guild Best Fringe Play Award, the 1996 Critics' Circle Award and the 1996 Evening Standard Award for Most Promising Playwright for **The Beauty Queen of Leenane**. Marina Carr won the 19th Susan Smith Blackburn Prize (1996/7) for **Portia Coughlan**. Conor McPherson won the 1997 George Devine Award, the 1997 Critics' Circle Award and the 1997 Evening Standard Award for Most Promising Playwright for **The Weir.** Ayub Khan-Din won the 1997 Writers' Guild Award for Best West End Play, the 1997 Writers' Guild New Writer of the Year Award and the 1996 John Whiting Award for **East is East**. Anthony Neilson won the 1997 Writers' Guild Award for Best Fringe Play for **The Censor**. The Royal Court was the overall winner of the 1995 Prudential Award for the Arts for creativity, excellence, innovation and accessibility. The Royal Court Theatre Upstairs won the 1995 Peter Brook Empty Space Award for innovation and excellence in theatre.

Now in its temporary homes, the Duke of York's and Ambassadors Theatres, during the two-year refurbishment of its Sloane Square theatre, the Royal Court continues to present the best in new work. After four decades the company's aims remain consistent with those established by George Devine. The Royal Court is still a major focus in the country for the production of new work. Scores of plays first seen at the Royal Court are now part of the national and international dramatic repertoire.

The Royal Court Theatre Bookshop

Located in the foyer of the Theatre Downstairs, the Royal Court Theatre bookshop is open most afternoons and evenings until after the evening performance.

It holds a wide range of theatre books, playtexts and film scripts - over 100 titles in all.

Many Royal Court Theatre playtexts are available for just £2. Among these are the recent productions of:

The Weir - Conor McPherson
I Am Yours - Judith Thompson
The Chairs - Eugène Ionesco
Never Land - Phyllis Nagy
Blue Heart - Caryl Churchill
The Censor - Anthony Neilson
East is East - Ayub Khan-Din
The Leenane Trilogy
(The Beauty Queen of Leenane
A Skull in Connemara
The Lonesome West)
- Martin McDonagh
Shopping and F£££ing
- Mark Ravenhill

The bookshop also sells polo shirts, record bags, mugs and chocolate.

Telephone enquiries can be made directly to the Bookshop Manager, Del Campbell, on 0171 565 5024.

**Royal Court Theatre Downstairs
St Martin's Lane
London
WC2N 4BG**

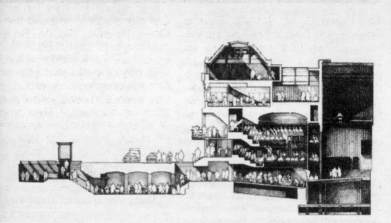

The Royal Court Theatre, Sloane Square
Architects Haworth Tompkins

DEVELOPMENT COMMITTEE

Elisabeth Murdoch
(Chair)
Julia Brodie
Timothy Burrill
Anthony Burton
Jonathan Cameron
Jonathan Caplan QC
Ronnie Cooke Newhouse
Chris Corbin
Robert Dufton
Stephen Gottlieb
Jan Harris
Susan Hayden
Angela Heylin

Malcolm Horsman
John Jay
David Liddiment
Hon. David McAlpine
Feona McEwan
Sonia Melchett
Helen Otton
Alan Parker
Maria Peacock
Carol Rayman
Angharad Rees
Ralph Simon
Sue Stapely
Charlotte Watcyn Lewis

We Need Your Support

The Royal Court Theatre, Sloane Square, was built in 1888 and is the longest-established theatre in England with the dedicated aim of producing new plays. We were thrilled to be awarded £16.2 million in September 1995 - from the National Lottery through the Arts Council of England - towards the complete renovation and restoration of our 100-year old home. This award has provided us with a unique opportunity to redevelop this beautiful theatre and building work is already underway at the Sloane Square site. However, in order to receive the full Lottery award, the Royal Court must raise almost £6 million itself as partnership funding towards the capital project.

The support of individuals, companies, charitable trusts and foundations is of vital importance to the realisation of the redevelopment of the Royal Court Theatre and we are very grateful to those who have already made a major contribution:

BSkyB Ltd
Double O Charity
Granada Group Plc
News International Plc
Pathé
Peter Jones
Quercus Charitable Trust
The Rayne Foundation
RSA Art for Architecture Award Scheme
Basil Samuel Charitable Trust
The Trusthouse Charitable Foundation
The Woodward Charitable Trust

Our campaign to re-build the Royal Court Theatre, Sloane Square, is meeting with tremendous success: on-site, exciting transformations have taken place in the past year and the first major milestone of the project has been achieved with the end of the excavation work. The completion of all the excavations represents a significant point in the development programme: from now on we start re-building the Royal Court in earnest.

Meanwhile, the Stage Hands campaign - which was launched with the aim of raising over £500,000 from audience members and the general public, towards our £6 million target - has also passed a major milestone. We've now raised over £260,000 in donations and pledges and we are grateful to our many supporters who have so generously donated to the appeal.

However, we still have some way to go to reach our goal and each donation keeps the building work at Sloane Square moving forward: for example, a donation of £20 pays for 40 bricks, a donation of £50 pays for cedar panelling for the auditorium and a donation of £100 pays for two square meters of reclaimed timber flooring.

If you would like to help, or for further information, please contact the Development Office on 0171 565 5050

Stage Hands Appeal

Royal Court Theatre

How the Royal Court is brought to you

The Royal Court (English Stage Company Ltd) is supported financially by a wide range of private companies and public bodies and earns the remainder of its income from the Box Office and its own trading activities.

The company receives its principal funding from the Arts Council of England, which has supported the Court since 1956. The Royal Borough of Kensington & Chelsea gives an annual grant to the Royal Court Young People's Theatre and the London Boroughs Grants Committee contributes to the cost of productions in the Theatre Upstairs.

Other parts of the company's activities are made possible by sponsorship and private foundation support:

1993 saw the start of our association with the A.S.K Theater Projects of Los Angeles, which is funding a Playwrights Programme at the Royal Court.

1997 marks the third Jerwood Foundation Jerwood New Playwrights series, supporting the production of new plays by young writer.

1997 also sees the first Barclays New Stages - Staging the New season, with four productions and a stage design conference, promoting the exploration of innovation in form and staging.

We are grateful to all our supporters for their vital and on-going commitment.

TRUSTS AND FOUNDATIONS
The Baring Foundation
The Campden Charities
John Cass's Foundation
The Chase Charity
The Esmeé Fairbairn
  Charitable Trust
The Robert Gavron
  Charitable Trust
Paul Hamlyn Foundation
The Jerwood Foundation
The John Lyons' Charity
The Mercers' Charitable
  Foundation
The Prince's Trust
Peggy Ramsay Foundation
The Lord Sainsbury Foundation
  for Sport & the Arts
The Basil Samuel Charitable Trust
The John Studzinski
  Foundation
The Wates Foundation
The Woodward Charitable Trust

SPONSORS
AT&T
Barclays Bank plc
Hugo Boss
The Granada Group plc
Marks & Spencer plc
Mishcon de Reya Solicitors
The New Yorker
Business Members
Channel Four Television
Chubb Insurance Company of
  Europe S.A.
Tomkins plc

PRIVATE SUBSCRIBERS
Patrons
Advanpress
Associated Newspapers Ltd
Bunzl plc
Citigate Communications
Criterion Productions plc
Greg Dyke
Homevale Ltd
Laporte plc
Lazard Brothers & Co. Ltd
Lex Service plc
Barbara Minto
New Penny Productions Ltd
Noel Gay Organisation
A T Poeton & Son Ltd
Greville Poke
Richard Pulford
Sir George Russell
The Simkins Partnership
Simons Muirhead and Burton
Richard Wilson
Benefactors
Mr & Mrs Gerry Acher
Bill Andrewes
Elaine Attias
Larry & Davina Belling
Angela Bernstein
Jeremy Bond
Katie Bradford
Julia Brodie
Julian Brookstone
Guy Chapman

Yuen-Wei Chew
Carole & Neville Conrad
Conway van Gelder
Coppard Fletcher & Co.
Lisa Crawford Irwin
Curtis Brown Ltd
Robyn Durie
Kim Fletcher & Sarah Sands
Winston Fletcher
Claire & William Frankel
Nicholas A Fraser
Norman Gerard
Henny Gestetner OBE
Carolyn Goldbart
Rocky Gottlieb
Stephen Gottlieb
Frank & Judy Grace
Jan Harris
Angela Heylin
Andre Hoffman
Chris Hopson
Juliet Horsman
Trevor Ingman
Institute of Practitioners
  in Advertising
International Creative
  Management
Peter Jones
Thomas & Nancy Kemeny
Sahra Lese
Judy Lever
Lady Lever
Sally Margulies
Mae Modiano
Sir Alan and Lady Moses
The Hon. Mrs A. Montagu
Pat Morton
Paul Oppenheimer
Michael Orr
Sir Eric Parker
Carol Rayman
Penny Reed
Angharad Rees
B J & Rosemary Reynolds
John Sandoe (Books) Ltd
Scott Tallon Walker
Nicholas Selmes
David & Patricia Smalley
Sue Stapely
Ann Marie Starr
Dr Gordon Taylor
A P Thompson
Elizabeth Tyson
Charlotte Watcyn Lewis
Nick Wilkinson

AMERICAN FRIENDS
Patrons
Miriam Blenstock
Tina Brown
Caroline Graham
Richard & Marcia Grand
Edwin & Lola Jaffe
Ann & Mick Jones
Maurie Perl
Rhonda Sherman
Members
Monica Gerard-Sharp
Linda S. Lese
Yasmine Lever
Leila Maw Strauss
Enid W. Morse
Gertrude Oothout
Mr & Mrs Frederick Rose
Mrs Paul Soros

Gas Station Angel

Characters

Manny
Mary Annie
Ace
Bron
Marshall
Bri
Gruff
Mati
Dyfrig
Mr Entertainment
Keith
Patsy
Policeman
Chambermaid
Janitor

Setting
Set in an ever fluid landscape but based on the remaining
half of a house whose other half has fallen into the sea.
Dislocated, unreal, fantastic, functional, witty and full of
possibility. Beds turn into cars, mountain becomes beach
airport becomes supermarket, this world the underworld,
shapes and structures bent and shaped to become
something else. Transformation is everything, magic and
invention vital. Dreams, myth and reality exist on the same
plane as long as the sky doesn't fall down to earth.

Note
This script went to print before the opening night and may
therefore differ slightly from the version performed.

Part One

Manny *wakes from a makeshift table in a sea of papers as* **Ace** *enters, rhythmically playing with a yo-yo. He stops.*

Ace   I saw a woman . . .

Manny   Where?

Ace   Down on the beach . . .

Manny   And?

Ace   She said to me . . .

Bron *enters.*

Bron   From where I was standing I thought you were dead.

Ace   I'm not dead.

Manny   Good boy.

Bron   I was on the verge of calling the emergency services when you shifted your position. Dead men don't change position I said to myself, so I came down to see if you were all right.

Ace   And I said I'm all right but things could be better.

Bron   I see.

Ace   Yes I said you see . . .

Bron   What?

Ace   Our house has fallen into the sea.

Bron   Fuck.

Ace   I know.

Bron   I'm sorry.

Ace   Forget it.

Bron   It must be terrible.

Ace   It is. (*Pause.*) It was once called a house in the country. Then it was called a house by the sea, then two weeks ago we had a bad storm and half our house fell into the sea and the other half stayed on land. I think it's called erosion. And then she said . . .

Bron   I've seen you before too.

Ace   Where?

Bron   Up on the cliff. Staring out at the sea.

Ace   When?

Bron   Long time ago now. I was with my brother.

Ace   I remember. It was summer.

Bron   Yes.

Ace   August the ninth.

Bron   I can't be sure of the date.

Ace   It was the ninth.

Bron   It could have been.

Ace   I keep a diary. I go out at night. I write down what I see. I like to think I see everything, but I obviously don't.

Bron   No.

Ace   Because until that night I'd never seen you before.

Bron   I see.

Ace   I'd like to think I'm the nightwatchman of this town but I suppose even a nightwatchman can't see everything.

Bron   Even nightwatchmen make mistakes.

Ace   They do.

Bron   I turned to my brother and said I can see a man.

Lights go up on **Marshall** *sitting at his fishing rod.*

Marshall   Where?

Bron Looking down on us.

Marshall Where?

Bron There, can you see him?

Marshall What's he doing out on the cliffs at this time
of night?

Bron Who knows.

Marshall It can't be Bri.

Bron No.

Marshall He doesn't look like Bri.

Bron No.

Marshall I'd like it to be Bri.

Bron And me.

Marshall But it isn't.

Bron No.

Marshall Bri wouldn't stand up on the cliffs in the dark.

Bron Unless . . .

Marshall He wouldn't, Bron, he wouldn't.

Bron He's gone now anyway.

Ace I went home.

Bron Maybe he's lost.

Ace To write in my diary what I saw.

Bron I wonder who he was.

Ace (*to* **Manny**) You were sitting at the table surrounded
by a sea of papers.

Manny 1961, 1971, 1981, 1991.

Bron Do you know him, Marshall?

Marshall I know his face.

Bron Who's his face?

Marshall Ace.

Bron Ace?

Marshall Ace. Hywel Ace. He's one of the Aces of Gaerlishe.

Bron Oh.

Marshall They say their house is going to fall into the sea.

Bron Their house?

Marshall Their house.

Bron The sea?

Marshall The sea, Bron, the fucking sea.

Manny Papers, journals, monthlies, weeklies, annuals, bi-annuals, comics, magazines and what for.

Ace To wrap our crockery in, Dad, what else.

Manny Crockery? Crockery? What the hell do you know about crockery?

Ace The council will come, Dad.

Manny The council, the council.

Ace They'll knock down our house.

Manny We'll keep an eye out for them.

Ace They'll come with warrants.

Manny We'll burn them.

Ace With eviction orders.

Manny We'll lock the door and won't let them in.

Ace They'll bring JCBs!

Manny OVER MY DEAD BODY. (*Pause.*) Did you see anyone out there?

Ace   In town?

Manny   On the mountains.

Ace   NO.

Manny   No one from the council snooping about?

Ace   No one.

Manny   Maybe it was the council that killed our chickens. If you see anyone from the council snooping around our chickens, you shoot first, ask questions later – capiche?

Ace   Our chickens are dead, Dad.

Manny   Capiche?

Ace   Capiche, Dad, capiche. (*Pause.*) And then . . .

Mary Annie *enters pedalling a chair and wearing an eye-mask.*

Mary Annie   Gurruga, gurruga, gurruga, no bell no lights can't see.

Ace   My mother woke up.

Mary Annie   Man? You there? I'm awake.

Manny   Mmm.

Mary Annie   I said I was awake.

Manny   I know.

Mary Annie   I haven't died.

Manny   No.

Mary Annie   Man?

Manny   What?

Mary Annie   I haven't died I said.

Manny   I heard.

Mary Annie   I'm still here.

Manny   Yes.

Pause.

Mary Annie   Man?

Manny   I'm listening.

Mary Annie   I can see the moon.

Manny   Good.

Mary Annie   It's lovely, go and have a look.

Manny   I'm busy.

Mary Annie   What you doing?

Manny   I was dozing.

Mary Annie   Liar.

Manny   I was reading then I was dozing.

Mary Annie   You're not in your chair.

Manny   I am.

Mary Annie   You're at the table.

Manny   I'm not.

Mary Annie   I can tell by your voice.

He moves back to the armchair.

Manny   I'm in the chair.

Mary Annie   Uh?

Manny   I'm in the chair.

Mary Annie   You moved.

Manny   No.

Mary Annie   Haven't you?

Manny   No, it's your ears.

Mary Annie   My external organs.

Manny   You've got to wait for them to hear right.

Mary Annie   Uh?

Manny   You've been sleeping on one and not the other.

Mary Annie   So?

Manny   So the one you haven't slept on hasn't been tampered with.

Mary Annie   Uh?

Manny   The one you've been sleeping on's been squashed ... so when you unsquash it, it takes quarter of an hour to hear properly through it.

Mary Annie   Oh.

Manny   That's why you thought I moved when I didn't.

Mary Annie   Because of my ears.

Manny   Yes.

Mary Annie   The good ear was listening one way and the sleeping ear was getting itself sorted out.

Manny   Yes.

Mary Annie   It was acclimatising to the new conditions.

Manny   Yes.

Mary Annie   Getting its bearings.

Manny   Yes.

Mary Annie   Under different circumstances.

Manny   Yes.

Mary Annie   Like us.

Manny   We're not moving.

Mary Annie   You did.

Manny   I never.

Mary Annie   It wasn't my ears.

Manny   It was.

Mary Annie You moved.

Manny No.

Pause.

Mary Annie We'll have to move. (*Pause.*) Man? We'll
have to move. They'll make us move.

Manny We're not moving nowhere.

Mary Annie They'll make us.

Manny They can make us much as they want but we're
not moving.

Mary Annie I don't want to move, Man.

Manny Nor me.

Mary Annie But we'll have to.

Manny No.

Mary Annie Our house will fall into the sea.

Manny So into the sea it will fall then.

Mary Annie But . . .

Manny We're not moving, Mary Annie.

Mary Annie Don't you Mary Annie me.

Manny I'll Mary Annie you as much as I want.

Mary Annie Huh.

Manny Mary Annie, Mary Annie, Mary Annie . . .

Mary Annie You never call me Wiff no more.

Manny Mary Annie.

Mary Annie Not since the monkey's parade.

Manny Mary Annie, Mary Annie, Mary Annie . . .

Mary Annie Only when you're angry. (*Pause.*) Mansell?
Why don't you call me Wiff no more? Like you used to.
(*Pause.*) Man? I like Wiff. Wiff is who I am. Wiff is the

mother of your child. (*Pause.*) Wiff is who I am. Wiff is me.
Awake. Looking up at the moon. Full moon. Me and the
fairies. Wiff and the fairies. (*Pause.*) Don't call me Mary
Annie, Man. Call me Wiff. (*Pause.*) Man? Man?

Manny Wiff.

Mary Annie Thank you, Manny, good old Manny,
brave old Manny stop the council moving us out before our
house falls into the sea. (*She laughs.*)

Ace (*to* **Bron**) The name's Ace, Hywel Ace, but most
people call me Ace.

Bron Bron.

Ace Growing up in a shrinking land next to a tantrum
sea hasn't been easy, Bron.

Bron I can imagine.

Ace Every day I came home from school to find our
house still standing was a victory. Small, but a victory is a
victory.

Lights change as we go back in time to young **Ace**, **Manny** *and*
Mary Annie *at the kitchen table.*

Manny If it carries on like this we'll lose half of Llanelli.

Mary Annie Which part?

Manny The ugly part.

Mary Annie Something good may come of it then.

Ace Is the sea going to eat our house, Dad?

Manny One day, boy, one day.

Mary Annie Eat your cabbage.

Ace On summer days when the sea was quiet I'd make
up stories. Fantastic stories. Life in storyland I could
control, the on-going war against the sea and real life I
couldn't.

Mary Annie *plays a hymn on a casio.*

Mary Annie   O Pam mae dicter o Myfanwy...

Manny   Will you stop that.

Mary Annie   It's Myfanwy.

Manny   I don't care if it's Shirley bloody Bassey, it's getting on my nerves.

Ace   And besides there were the fairies to think about.

At the table **Mary Annie** *is making Welsh cakes with young* **Ace**.

Ace   What happens when we die, Mam?

Mary Annie   Mm?

Ace   Do we go to Heaven?

Mary Annie   Maybe.

Ace   Where's Heaven?

Mary Annie   In the sky above the clouds.

Ace   Can you see Heaven from a plane?

Mary Annie   Who knows.

Ace   Can we go on a plane to find out?

Mary Annie   One day.

Ace   Can we go today?

Mary Annie   Not today, we got too much to do, pass me the sultanas.

Ace   I love Welsh cakes I do, with loads of currants and sultanas.

Mary Annie   So do the fairies.

Ace   Where do fairies live?

Mary Annie   Under the ground.

Ace   In Hell?

Mary Annie   No, who told you that?

Ace I don't know, but Heaven is in the sky and Hell is down below the ground.

Mary Annie Hell is somewhere else.

Ace Where?

Mary Annie Just somewhere else, that's all.

Ace That's what I think too, Mam, otherwise why would they put mamgu and tadcu in the ground. In Hell, they never done nothing wrong.

Mary Annie No.

Ace We put them in the ground so they can be with the fairies then?

Mary Annie Mmm . . .

Ace With Jesus and God. Is God a fairy, Mam?

Mary Annie God is a bad man.

Lights up on a graveyard where four small simple white crosses can be seen. **Mary Annie** *puts flowers on them.*

Mary Annie He took away four little angels before you came alone.

Ace Angels?

Mary Annie They would have been your brothers and sisters, but they were born with no breath. God took the breath away before they were born.

Ace So who gave me breath, Mam?

Mary Annie The fairies. I let them into my heart when God left me barren. You were a baby made by fairies, they came up from the underworld and put their hands on my belly. I saw them dance.

Music can be heard as we see fairies, angels and succubae dance.

Mary Annie Magical things can still happen in this cruel world, see. You've just got to know where to look, that's all.

Ace   So I believed. In stories and mysteries and magic.
Stories were good. Life had the sea and the council.

The angels and succubae evaporate as **Manny** *enters with a letter.*

Manny   'Regrettably, I have to inform you that the
demolition of your property at a date convenient to
yourselves is the only realistic solution. As I said in my
letter dated March twelfth, surveyors' reports indicate that
the cliff fronting your property are in a dangerously
unstable condition, and any anti-erosion measures taken by
this Council at this stage would not and indeed could not
remedy the situation. Whilst I have every sympathy for you
and your family's predicament I feel that I must endorse
the decision made at Council, and firmly believe we are
taking the safest and most cost-effective course of action.
Yours sincerely, D. Watkins.'

Ace   Bastards.

Mary Annie   Revenge that's what it is.

Manny   For what, we haven't got no quarrel with the
council.

Mary Annie   I'm not talking about the council . . . I'm
talking about them.

Manny   Who?

Mary Annie   Them . . . Them under the ground, under
the sea, under our feet, digging away, having parties,
wanting revenge.

Ace   Who, Mam?

Mary Annie   The bloody fairies, the tylwyth teg. Your
father dug up the field where they dance, now they won't
come out.

Manny   Don't be so soft, woman.

Mary Annie   I'm not being soft, it's not the council we
got to be afraid of, it's them. The council can't do nothing
because it's our land, they can't chuck us out, but as for

the fairies ... and the sea ... that's a different matter.

Manny There are no fairies, mun.

Mary Annie I've seen them with my own eyes, my mother's seen them and her mother before that, they used our field, they danced on it till your father ploughed it all up, but they won't dance again till they've had their revenge on us. It's not the council we got to be afraid of, it's the fairies. They're in cahoots with the sea.

Ace There's always a time when you try and pinpoint the exact moment when things change. Like a commentator in a football match always asks if this or that incident is the significant moment, the point at which A wins and B loses. In our house it was getting the council letter. For mam it was the last straw.

Mary Annie I'm going to bed to wait. I'm not getting up till we move into a caravan and the fairies have had our house.

She exits.

Manny We got to keep an eye on her.

Ace I know.

Manny In the meantime we write back to the council telling them to bugger off and we're not moving nowhere. If they want to try and get us out they'll have to burn us out. From now on we're on a twenty-four-hour vigil.

Ace Vigil?

Manny *grabs a gun.*

Manny Vigil. Anyone you see walking the hills in a suit and tie you tell me about. Capiche?

Ace Not all the council wear ties mun, Dad.

Manny Capiche?

Lights change back to **Ace** *and* **Bron** *on the beach.*

Bron Capiche?

Ace   That's what he said, means understand in Italian . . . or Spanish.

Manny   Edward G. Robinson used to say it in gangster films.

Ace   This is my story, Dad.

Manny   I'm sorry, I'm sorry . . . continue.

Ace   And then we stood there in silence watching the waves come in. I watched her push a stick into a dead jellyfish.

Manny   Then?

Ace   Then right out of the blue she said . . .

Bron   Would you like to come for a drive with me?

Manny   A drive?

Ace   In her car.

Bron   Because I've had a shitty day too. Maybe you want to come for a ride with me. I got a tinted glass blue Marina 1800 TC ready to drive into the heart of Saturday night.

Ace   And I said that sounds great.

Bron   Good. So let's drive.

Ace   And so we drove. I didn't care where. Some people are born lucky; others are born to lose. I want me and Bron to be the lucky ones. In sixteen hours forty-eight minutes she's turned my world upside down and I know in my bones things are never going to be the same again.

Manny   Marina?

Music plays as the set transforms into the James family's white-trash world. **Mati** *and* **Bron** *enter.*

Mati   Bloody music.

Bron   What music?

Mati On the TV.

Bron What music?

Mati *Sportsnight* with bloody Coleman, did you hear it?

Bron I heard it, yeh.

Mati I switched it off. I had to switch it off, I know we paid a lot for the aerial, but I had to switch it off. Bloody hate sport.

Bron It's not called that any more.

Mati What isn't?

Bron *Sportsnight* with Coleman.

Mati Uh?

Bron *Sportsnight* is now called with Desmond Lynam.

Mati Who's he?

Bron The older woman's crumpet.

Mati Crumpet?

Bron Tall, mid-forties, moustache, grey hair, just started wearing glasses.

Mati Never heard of him, and anyway, I switched it off as soon as I heard the music. Bloody music, bloody sport, bloody senseless kicking sweetbreads blown up round the field.

Bron What?

Mati That's what they used to be made of, innit?

Bron Bladders, Mam.

Mati Uh?

Bron Pig's bladders, not sweetbreads and anyway they're made of plastic now.

Mati Shows how much I know but who cares, it's still bloody stupid, running around after a ball in the rain, on a

Saturday afternoon, bootlaces, blood, bloody bandages and all for what? For a few pints in the club on a Saturday night, looking forward to the strippers on a Sunday with her fags and her oil to pour over herself from a Windolene bottle, I know, I seen them.

Bron   When?

Mati   Lorraine told me. I never been myself, it's men only. She gave it a go for a bit on a part-time basis, but the men didn't like the Windolene bottle, told her to get baby oil in a real baby-oil bottle, she packed it in after that.

Bron   Lost her bottle, did she?

Mati   You'd think with all the sprogs that she's got she wouldn't find getting a baby-oil bottle a problem. Five she's got, all under eight too. What did you say?

Bron   I'll have to remember that.

Mati   Remember what you want it's all bloody stupid, nothing makes sense to me no more. I mean look at your father, he still drinks in the Ship and Pilot even though they've ripped the guts out of the place. All he's ever done since whatsisname modernised it is complain. Why don't he go somewhere else, innit?

The father, **Gruff***, enters.*

Gruff   Because the Ship's the place I've always drunk, Mati, and my father did, and his father before that.

Mati   But you don't like it no more.

Gruff   Like it? It's bastard terrible.

Mati   But they say all the furnishings are Laura Ashley.

Gruff   Laura Ashley be buggered, it's a pub not a bastard country kitchen pretending to be a country kitchen with flowers and curtains and fancy little alcoves with plasterboard and ply, it's all crap. And it's not even wood.

It's fucking joke wood. WHO THE FUCK ARE THEY
TRYING TO KID?

Enter **Mr Entertainment** *as we go to the Ship and Pilot pub.*

Mr Entertainment If you don't like it, why don't you
piss off down the road?

Gruff Don't worry, I'm going, I'm going. Fuck your beer,
fuck your pub. FUCK YOU!

Gruff *exits.*

Mr Entertainment Miserable git, who the fuck wants
people like that in the place? Pub was dying 'til I got hold
of it. Old fuckers drinking three pints and pissing over the
floor of the toilet. No music. No crack. TV on in the
corner, fucking dominoes with faded dots. Dotless
dominoes, wonder them old fuckers could see them. Play
from memory half of them did. Put a penny on the pint
they go on strike. Drink stout from a bottle, well, them days
are gone. Them days are fucking gone. I got the new Ship
and the old Ship, not a domino in sight – new Ship for the
youngsters and the dull fuckers. Bingo six thirty to seven
thirty, then karaoke from eight 'til half nine, rave disco
with an extended licence 'til one o'clock, fucking lovely,
fucking gorgeous, E-ed out, bottled water, bubbly water,
that's when I bring it out, goes like fuck with the
youngsters too when the dull fuckers take E and whisky,
shag their brains completely. But I don't care, I got Honest
Bri on the door to sort out the fighting, my daughter Cindy
running the fucking fish-and-chip shop – we are raking it
in. FUCKING RAKING WE ARE. MR
ENTERTAINMENT, THAT'S ME. But I got to go, the
bingo's about to start. Call in if you're passing. We'll
always keep a welcome. And remember, you'll have a
FUCKING BALL. RIGHT, YOU SUCKERS, EYES
DOWN FOR A FULL HOUSE. LET'S BE HAVING
YOU.

He exits.

Mati But he keeps going there.

Bron   Habit.

Mati   Habit, habit. 'Bout time he changed his bloody habits, cos if he's not in the Ship he's in work, bloody Ship, bloody work, between the two of them I never see him. I tell you, Bron, I can't take no more, it's all gone nuts, it's all gone crazy, nothing makes sense any more, the world's darts don't reach all the way to the dartboard any more.

She exits.

Bron *sits at a check-out counter in the supermarket.*

Bron   And I suppose she's got a point too but this town is no different to loads of other towns around the place, around the world if it comes to that, and this family's just the same too, give or take a few things. I mean we may be on the extreme side of things but the principle's the same. Secrets and lies. A fucked-up past. Maybe if we faced up to the past then maybe we wouldn't find the world so confusing.

*A supervisor (***Keith***) enters and leans close to* **Bron** *as she works.*

Keith   Everything all right, check-out one?

Bron   Yes thanks, just fine.

An element of sexual harassment is evident in this exchange. **Bron** *resents it,* **Keith** *loves it.* **Keith** *smiles knowingly.*

Keith   Good . . . good.

Bron   But it ain't easy. I mean, how do I explain my brother Bri, or my brother Marshall. Or come to that, my boss Keith?

Bron *swings her bag on to her shoulder and turns to exit the staff room when* **Keith** *blocks her. He is too close for comfort.*

Keith   Flying solo tonight?

Bron   Listen, Keith. When a woman takes a pack of Coco-Pops home with her at night, it's a pretty sure sign that she wants to be alone.

Keith Bitch.

Bron A cryptic comment is the only way to leave a nobody supermarket supervisor in smalltown. It preserves a woman's mystery, gives her that distance, that possibility. It makes people long into their feathery beds what a girl like me is doing in a place like this. And the answer? Family.

A car starts up and we hear it pull away. **Bron** *exits as the supermarket clears to reveal* **Bri** *standing alone.*

Bri Crack. The sound of wood snapping. It's the first thing I remember. Then nothing. Then a splash. I must have been about ten. Bron was seven and Marsh must have been about seven.

Bron Has Batman got nipples?

Bri Yes.

Bron How do you know?

Marshall Cos he's a man, Bron.

Bron He's a bat.

Bri He's a man who turns into a bat when there's trouble.

Marshall That's why they call him Batman.

Bron But not a real bat?

Bri No. A man with a bat's special powers.

Marshall Bats hang upside down in caves.

Bri In the night.

Marshall They come out at night.

Bron But they can't drive cars?

Marshall No.

Bron Only people drive cars.

Marshall Yeh.

Bron Do bats have nipples?

Marshall Uh?

Bron Bri?

Bri No.

Bron Neither has Batman.

Marshall He has.

Bron So he can't be a man.

Bri Batman's a man, Bron, and men have nipples.

Bron So why can't I see them?

Marshall Cos he's wearing his bat costume, if you took off his costume you'd see his nipples.

Bron But it won't come off, he's not like Action Man, you can take off Action Man's costume, see – look.

Marshall Who told you you could play with my Action Man?

Bron I wasn't playing with him.

Marshall So how do you know you can take off his costume?

Bron Stop it, Marshall, I was only . . . Tell him, Bri, he's picking on me.

Bri He's not.

Bron He is. I haven't touched his Action Man. I was only . . .

Bri So what's it doing in your hand, Bron?

Bron I was only showing you, that's all.

Marshall Give him here.

Bron No.

Marshall Give him here.

Snatches it from her.

Bron   Bully. I hate you, Marshall James. I'm never going to play with you again.

Bron *walks into the shadows.*

Bri   Bron ran back to the house, leaving me and Marshall talking. I was close to him them. Me and him were inseparable. That day out of the blue I grabbed his hand and cut his finger with a knife.

Marshall   Ahh . . . what you do that for?

Bri *cuts his finger and joins it to his brother's.*

Bri   Me and you are blood brothers now, Marsh.

Marshall   Uh.

Bri   Means we'll always look after each other, right.

Marshall   Right . . . but we're already brothers, Bri, I got your blood in me already.

Bri   It's the ritual, Marsh, the ritual. And we went down to the rocks at the foot of the estuary. We made ourselves a batcave. In the roots of an old tree. The tide was coming in but we were two batmen in search of sanctuary, too busy on a mission to notice. Marsh went first, climbing into the roots of the tree. Then I heard the crack of snapping wood. Then . . . saw him fall.

Marshall   I went under. My feet touched the bottom. I looked up, the sun streaming in through the green water. I could see Bri's red jumper. I went back up, tried to shout but nothing came out, only water, I went under again, something pulling me down, deeper and deeper. I don't remember any panic. Just peace. I looked up again. I saw a stick come through the surface.

Bri   Grab hold of it, grab hold of it . . .

Marshall   But I couldn't reach.

Bri   MARSHALL. MARSHALL . . .

Marshall   I was moving further away. I couldn't see the stick any more and I couldn't see Bri. I was on my own. In my wellingtons, trousers and a green jumper with a Batman badge. I wasn't afraid. It was peaceful. Sometimes I wish I could have stayed there. Under the green water. Looking up at the sun. Floating for ever and for ever. Dead.

Lights come up on **Bron** *and* **Mati** *in the house.* **Bri** *runs in breathless.*

Bri   Quick, quick, it's Marshall. He's fallen in.

Mother   What?

Bri   In the river, he couldn't reach . . . HURRY, MAM, HURRY, HURRY!

Mati *and* **Bri** *exit.* **Bron** *remains alone.*

Bron   I never moved. I don't know why. Maybe it was shock. The next thing I can remember is jumping up and down hysterical until dad came and shook me telling me to stop.

Gruff *enters in his abattoir clothes.*

Gruff   I was just coming in. I heard Bron screaming and I saw Bri and Mati run down towards the river. By the time I got to the river everything was over.

Mati   He was floating towards the sea. On his back. He looked peaceful. I loved him. He was my son. I walked straight into the river.

Bri   But I knew mam couldn't swim. I stood on the bank watching my mother and brother drown.

Mati   I reached him and held up his head. I don't think I panicked. I wanted to die with him. I loved him. He was my son.

Bri   Then out of nowhere two people came. Strangers I'd never seen before, a man and a woman. They dived in, pulling out my mother and brother. Mam was still breathing but Marshall was dead. The man kept shouting save the woman, save the woman, the boy's lost. The woman stopped trying to save Marshall and helped the man save mam. I looked at Marshall lying dead on the bank. His heart had stopped beating. I could hear mam coughing and bringing up water. Then I don't know why, but I kissed him. Harder and harder, I blew air into his mouth, harder and harder, I pushed at his chest and I kissed him harder and harder and then his chest moved and I tasted water. He was alive.

Gruff The strangers helped Mati back to the house, I carried Marshall in my arms, they called the doctor and by the time he came, colour was coming back into Marsh's body. He was blue. Except round his belly button. He was going to live.

Bri He was still unconscious but the doctor said he'd be all right. He had to give Bron an injection for shock. People came from the other houses to see if we were all right too. Mam sat with a blanket by the fire and then she said . . .

Mati Where is the man and the woman?

Bri And everyone looked round, but there was no sign of them.

Mati Who were they and where did they come from, Bri?

Bri I don't know, Mam, I've never seen them before.

Mati We never had a chance to thank them for what they've done.

Bri But we never heard from them. Dad tried to find out who they were, but nobody knew.

Gruff Angels.

Bri Said my father.

Bron Fairies.

Bri Said Bron. But nobody knew.

Gruff He wasn't meant to die, that's all. Someone was looking after him. Marshall James is a very lucky boy.

Mati He's a special boy.

Gruff Special.

Bri And I watched them look at him in his bed. I heard them tend to him as he threw up the dregs of the river all night. He wasn't just Marshall James no more. He was special. He was Jesus. He was an angel. They told him he was. He had a future. They all thought so. Mam, dad, Bron. Nobody said anything to me. I never made the papers. 'Strangers save mother and son in estuary drama' said the headline. They all forgot me. I kissed him back to life that night and nobody gave me the credit for it. The strangers saw it, but they disappeared. I tried to tell dad what happened but he just said . . .

Gruff We all know what happened, Bri, now don't tell lies. Lying will get you nowhere in this world.

Bri So I said no more about it. He was my brother before that day. My blood brother. And now he wasn't. He was special. And I hated him for it. Drowning would have preserved my love for him. Living made love impossible. It moved the goal posts. I should have let him die. Why the fuck didn't I let him die? I lost a brother that day and I still fucking miss him.

Bron Things were never the same in our house after that. Marshall got the angel treatment with milk and Jaffa Cakes on the settee. I carried on trying to think everything was normal when I knew in my bones it wasn't and Bri became the black sheep of the family, simple as that. What foxed me was that it was our angel Marshall not Bri who axed twenty-four of Dyfrig's lambs to death two and a half years ago. Never touched the ewes, only the lambs. Very dark, very strange, very Welsh.

Marshall I did it cos I didn't fit in. Mrs Conti said.

Bron She ran Conti's Café in the Square. Known as

Conti in Italy but Sonti in Wales. I put it down to the
Methodists.

Marshall I walked into the caff. Jocks's on the square. I
pushed the door open, heard the bell ring, saw Jock's ma
look up from behind the sweets, saw the boys watching
Paula then watching me. His fingers still on the flipper, the
silver ball hanging in time, the machine waiting for me to
say something. Paula waiting for me to say something. The
boys waiting for me to say something. Jock's ma in mid sup
of her sweet waiting for me to say something . . . so I said
it. All right, Paula, how's it going like and I slapped him
on the back, the ball flew past the flippers, Paula turns and
calls me a fucking wanker. Game over. He holds me up
against the wall. His face is red, you prick, he says, you
stupid fucking prick. Then he butts me. I go down. Paula
walks out, the boys follow. I see them through blurred,
watery eyes. My nose bleeds. Jock's ma comes over to me
with a tissue, here, she says, wipe your face. I wipe my
face. I'm sorry . . . I say. But I really try, Mrs Conti . . . I
really try. You don't fit in, boy, that's your trouble. Your
words is wrong. Your language. Here, wipe your face. I
wipe my face. Why innit? Fucking why? What do you say,
Bri?

Bri *doesn't respond.*

Lights go up on **Mati** *and* **Gruff**.

Gruff Why?

Mati Why?

Gruff When he had everything going for him. How can
they call him a psychopath if he's got hobbies?

Mati Who knows.

Gruff I mean HE CAN TIE FUCKING FLIES.
COCHABONDEES.

Mati Maybe we spoilt him.

Gruff Spoilt him? He was special, mun, Mati, he died

then he came back to life. He was like fucking Jesus.

Mati Don't swear.

Gruff He didn't come back to life to axe Dyfrig's new-born lambs to death, did he? Did he?

Mati No.

Gruff So how am I ever going to show my face in the Ship from now on?

Mati You hate the Ship.

Gruff I'll have to drink in the bastard Butch now, fucking hell, fucking, fucking hell.

He exits.

Mati (*to* **Bri**) And what are you looking at? It wasn't my fault. None of it is my fault.

Bri No.

Mati I've loved you as much as I've loved your brother.

Bri Yeh.

Mati Wasn't me who called him an angel. It was your father.

Bri I know. (*Pause.*) Mam?

Mati What?

Bri I've bought a new car.

Mati You stupid bugger, on whose money?

Bri It didn't cost much. I can do it up.

Mati But we already got a car, your father's car.

Bri I know but I wanted a car I can call my own. I'd like us to go for a drive in it, me, you, dad, Bron, Marshall, all of us.

Mati What for?

Bri Because I got something I want to tell you.

Mati Tell me now.

Bri Now isn't the time, Mam. I want to tell everyone the same time. And not in this house. Somewhere else.

Mati Like where?

Bri Somewhere.

Mati Somewhere?

Bri Yeh.

Mati I'll see what your father says. I'm off to the bingo. See you after.

Mati *exits.*

Bron But we never went on that trip, not as a family anyway. Me and Bri went to the airport once, that's all. Then three days later he was banned for drink-driving. He never drove that car again.

Lights up on a prison cell.

Bri I'm not a sad fucking bastard. I'm not a suicide. I'm not a beam swinger. I'm not a piece of shit … I am not a piece of old rope, I ain't hung, I AIN'T FUCKING DEAD. I ain't the circus, I ain't the act, I ain't the flying trapeze. I'm Brian Fucking James. I drive a blue tinted glass Marina 1800 TC into the heart of Saturday night, you fucks.

Policeman Did.

Bri What?

Policeman Did.

Bri Uh?

Policeman Drive a Marina. Blow test positive. Piss test positive, blood test positive. Three-card trick. Put an advert in the *Echo*, motoring. Thursdays. You're nicked. (*He slams door.*)

Bri *sits in the cell.*

Bron   And that's the last time we saw him. He walked out of the police station and disappeared into thin air. At first we thought he'd gone on walkabout and lost all track of time. I mean Bri was useless with time and he went off for a couple of weeks without telling anyone before that. Turned out he'd been to Old Trafford to watch Man. United play, then the cops found him wandering around the perimeter fence of the airport and brought him home. But he was different. And Marshall was different and the house was different. Everything was different. And I was different too. Some people think he's dead. (**Bri** *laughs.*) Some people say they've seen him. (**Bri** *laughs.*) Some people say he's gone with Gunn to Australia to deliver pizzas in Queensland. But nobody knows.

Bri   Nobody knows, nobody knows.

Bri *exits laughing.*

Bron   Two years is a long time. Dad and Marshall don't go fishing together any more. Mam still can't work out why the world's darts don't reach the dartboard any more, and I moved to town for my job because I didn't want people to talk any more. (*Pause.*) I got to keep the blue tinted glass Marina 1800 TC that I like to drive into the heart of Saturday night.

Ace *enters.*

Ace   August the ninth. Summer. A heat wave the day I first saw her.

Sound of a car revving up and pulling away. Lights change to a park, the atmosphere throbs with jungle music and youth.

Ace   Teenagers drink Hooch in the park. Not dark yet. I hear them argue about labels, designer labels.

Voice 1   Bilabong.

Voice 2   Swatch.

Voice 3   Animal.

Voice 4   Armani.

Voice 1   Hugo fuckin' Boss.

Voice 2   Slag.

Voice 3   Donna Karan.

Voice 4   Nike.

Voice 1   Cunting Adidas.

Voice 2   Reebok.

Voice 3   Gucci.

Voice 4   Puma.

Voice 1   Calvin Bastard Klein.

Voice 2   Pants, perfume or both?

Voice 1   Who cares. IT'S A NAME AND IT'S ALL IN THE NAME!

Voice 2   YOUR NAME AIN'T CALVIN FUCKING KLEIN. It's Adrian Parry.

Voice 1   Fuck off.

Voice 2   Fuck off yourself.

Ace   They fight, they make up, they fight again, drink Hooch, share E. Get warm. The watered Es lie back and look up at the stars. The E-less only drunk start to bicker and move away.

Voice 3   Leighton. (*Pause.*) Lei ... gh ... ton.

Voice 4   Come on if you're coming.

Voice 3   I'm coming, I'm coming.

Voice 4   So fucking 'urry up, mun.

Voice 3   I am 'urrying I am. Do you love me?

Voice 4   Uh?

Voice 3   You heard.

Voice 4   For fuck's sake, Patsy mun.

Voice 3   Because I FUCKING LOVE YOU, YOU
SHED. (*Pause.*) Leighton ... wait ... LEIGHTON!

Ace   But Leighton drives away on a Kawasaki 125.
Leighton's lover, Patsy, less than a beauty joins the other
E-less now smoking Regal at the foot of the H. Patsy gets
drunk and sad. She's only seventeen but already the prison
bars are crowding her head.

Patsy   I ain't got no roots. I ain't got no morality. I ain't
got no religion. I ain't got no family. I ain't got no values.
I ain't got no hopes. I ain't got no desires but you know
the worst of it is, man ... ?

Voice 4   What?

Patsy   I ain't got no dreams.

Voice 4   Straight up?

Patsy   Straight up. I don't know what the fuck's happened
to them, man, but they ain't up there in my head no more.

Voice 4   Where did they go, Patsy?

Patsy   Go?

Voice 4   Yeh, man, like where did they go to?

Patsy   They never went anywhere, man, they were never
there in the first place.

Voice 4   That's heavy.

Patsy   That's true.

Voice 4   You must want something.

Patsy   Wanting and dreaming are two different things,
man, I mean I want to win the Lottery but I don't dream
about it, a: because I probably won't win it, and b: if I win
it, it still won't be dreaming, man, it'll be real and the
problem is that what's real ... what's real right, what's real
right ... (*Pause.*) I hate the real me. All that's real is a
heap of shit, man. Real means shopping, shitting, bleeding,
freezing, boiling, all the things you have to put up with.

I've had it with putting up with things, man. Putting up with things. Fuck it. Fuck all of it.

Voice 4 Dying?

Patsy Dying? What's that?

Voice 4 Means . . .

Patsy I know what it means man, and I couldn't give two fucks 'bout it. Dying means end game exit. Stop. No go. End. Bra-fucking-vo.

Voice 4 So?

Patsy So?

Voice 4 So what's the answer?

Patsy Who gives a fuck. Just give me the fucking drugs. (*She grabs the stuff off him. Takes two.*) Now fuck me. Fuck my cunt, my head, my mouth, my arse, my nose, my ears, my eyes, my fucking everything. (*He doesn't move.*) Fuck me Baz. (*Pause.*) Fuck me. FUCK ME!

Ace And they fuck. Somewhere in the bushes by the river. The man from number 48 passes, dragging his dog Tyson for a walk. A ritual. I spoke to him once. Said he worked for the railways. Said if it wasn't for his dog he'd . . . his eyes filled up. I looked away. I just love the dog he says. (*Pause.*) I cross the road and over the Teddy Bear bridge up to the mountains behind Pelican, overlooking the sea. I roll myself a spliff and look down at the waves. I see a bloke fishing at first. I can't make him out then I see it's Marshall James, the axeman of the innocent. Dyfrig the Garth once told me he lost a new season's flock.

Enter **Dyfrig** *into a hell of a Ship and Pilot disco bar.*

Dyfrig Terrible things are being done to our sheep, Ace.

Ace I know, Dyf, I know.

Dyfrig They're the future of the flock, Ace.

Ace I know, Dyf, I know.

Dyfrig   Slaughtered and still wet they are, Ace.

Ace   It's terrible, Dyf, terrible.

Dyfrig   If I catch whoever's doing it, Ace, I'll blow their fucking brains out with both barrels.

Ace   I know, Dyf.

Dyfrig   I wouldn't ask no questions, Ace.

Ace   No.

Dyfrig   I wouldn't hesitate.

Ace   No.

Dyfrig   Blam fuckin' blam. I'd watch him drop like a stone. You wouldn't know nothing about it, would you, Ace?

Ace   Come off it, Dyf, that isn't my line. I'm an erudite fucker.

Dyfrig   Like into glue?

Ace   No, Dyf.

Dyfrig   Do you sniff it, like Locktite?

Ace   No, Dyf, it's just a word.

Dyfrig   A word, right.

Ace   Words are beautiful, Dyf, they conjure up things.

Dyfrig   Like a magician?

Ace   Yeh ... like take the word docile ...

Dyfrig   Docile ...

Ace   Don't you think that's a fucking perfect word?

Dyfrig   In what way perfect?

Ace   In what it conjures up ... let it run over your tongue, Dyf ... d ... o ... c ... ile, try it. D ... o ... c ... ile ...

Dyfrig   D ... o ... c ... ile ...

Ace   What you reckon?

Dyfrig   I reckon it's all right.

Ace   All right, fuckin' hell, Dyf, it was BEAUTIFUL.

Dyfrig   Keep your fucking voice down, Ace, we don't want everyone to hear.

Ace   Why not, Dyf, don't you like people to know you play with words?

Dyfrig   Only words I know.

Ace   Like what?

Dyfrig   Fuck off.

Ace   What else.

Dyfrig   Shag.

Ace   You like that, Dyf.

Dyfrig   And cunt.

Ace   Cunt.

Dyfrig   Cunt. Women's cunts. And lips and arse ... and cock.

Ace   Cock.

Dyfrig   Cock and cunt.

Ace   They go together.

Dyfrig   Yeh. In and out.

Ace   That's beautiful, Dyf.

Dyfrig   I know.

Ace   I can see your mind looking at the picture ... you're dreaming, man. One word and all of a sudden you're there ... fucking.

Dyfrig   Yeh.

Ace   In and out.

Dyfrig   Yeh.

Ace   Fast and slow.

Dyfrig   Yes, Ace, yes.

Ace   Faster and faster.

Dyfrig   Yeh.

Ace   Slower and slower.

Dyfrig   Fu-uck.

Ace   You're on the edge, Dyf.

Dyfrig   I know, man, I know.

Ace   So is she.

Dyfrig   Yeh.

Ace   She's screaming, Dyf.

Dyfrig   Yeh.

Ace   And you are.

Dyfrig   Yeh.

Ace   In and out, in and out, faster and faster and faster and faster and FASTER AND FASTER AND YOU'RE THERE DYF FUCKING RELEAAAASED.

Dyfrig *screams at the top of his voice. The other people in the pub stare at him. They put down their glasses, the music cuts, then silence.* **Dyfrig** *slowly recovers, breathless. He looks around at the shocked faces. He gets up. Looks around him.*

Pause.

Dyfrig   I am beautiful. I am fucking beautiful. (*Pause.*) You might not be able to see it ... but I am. It's written all over my face. But nobody can see it, only Ace. When I step out on to the street people say there he goes. What an ugly bastard. His past is only acne and boils. Fuck how he must have worried as a boy. Poor boy, pity poor boy, farmer boy.

Voice 1   He's got the face of an unexploded experiment.

Dyfrig   Yes.

Voice 1   Chemical

Dyfrig   Yes.

Voice 2   Volatile.

Dyfrig   Yes.

Voice 1   Unstable.

Dyfrig   Yes.

Voice 1   Unwatchable.

Dyfrig   Yes, yes, yes, say it, say it, say it. FUCKING
SAY IT. DON'T BEAT ABOUT THE BASTARD BUSH!

Voice 1   Unkissable.

Dyfrig   Yeeeeessss . . . (*Pause.*) Unkissable (*Pause.*) I
watched angels undress through broken glass. A state
school. Run down. Unboarded. The chaste hid behind
raincoats. The confident chattered as they took off ties and
shirts and skirts. They bent down to tie shoelaces. I licked
my unkissable lips. Mouths are a weakness in our family.
Ulcers, cold sores, braces, extractions, fillings. A love of
confectionery. A sweet shop. The changing room. Through
broken glass the sweets of changing girls. Making women.
Not looking at me. Looking through me. Beyond. I could
have licked and sucked at their bodies. I would have put
my damaged head through broken glass for them. But
didn't. I did when I got the courage but by then the
changing room was empty. School was out. Only me and
the janitor remained.

Janitor *enters.*

Janitor   You got the face of a chemical experiment, boy.

Dyfrig   I know.

Janitor   Have you tried alcohol.

Dyfrig   Yes.

Janitor   Not in a glass, in a bowl.

Dyfrig   Bowl?

Janitor   Jameson's. Pour in the bottle in a bowl. Then put in your head. Hold it in there for as long as you dare. Then repeat.

Dyfrig   I did as he said.

Janitor   If you can't change the future of a man's face, what chance society?

Janitor *exits.*

Dyfrig *puts his head in a bowl and screams.*

Dyfrig   Fuck. Gulled, me. By a janitor, what do I do. The sweets have left the sweetshop for their tea, only me. I mean I remain. Who the fuck am I? A boy? A farmer's boy. A man? A half man? Beast? Angel? Demon? Member of the underworld? Men who leave prison and change their appearance? Plastic surgery. Did they begin by putting poisoned heads in Irish whiskey? While still wearing prison clothes? While still on the run? Is Ronnie Biggs the great sixties train robber a different man in Brazil than he was in London town when he cavorted on the beach with Sid and Johnny, the Sex Pistols. Who killed Bambi? Did he begin his transformation by putting his head in whiskey? Before dyeing his hair? Growing a moustache? Changing the geography of his face? How will we shed rocks to become men in the twenty-first century? (*Pause.*) Uh? (*Pause.*) Uh? These are the things I think about when you all pass me in the street, see. I'm not ugly. I am beautiful. (*Pause.*) But none of you notice. (*Pause.*) Only Ace. Hywel Ace, whose house one day will fall into the sea. The chronicler of these times. Tonight will appear in his DIARY, won't it, Ace?

Ace   Sure thing, Dyf.

Dyfrig   Home he'll go, write it all in. Record it. August

the ninth. Summer. Hope the sea won't get it when it
comes. Lose it. I hope they'll find it in the ruins of his
house. Stuffed into his album sleeves. His records. Because
we were before records. Vinyl forgot us. A chronicle of
smalltown. Small thoughts. Small heads. But not all of us.
(*Pause.*) Some of us are beautiful. Not only me. But you
can't see it. (*Pause.*) You can't see it. You just can't see it.
(*Pause.*) Let me get pregnant by the spunk of a fairy I say.
From the underground. The otherworld. Then you might
think me beautiful. (*Pause.*) Good night, Ace.

Ace   Good night, Dyf.

Dyfrig   Good night, all.

Dyfrig *exits in silence, shutting the door.*

Voice 1   Well.

Voice 2   Well, well.

Voice 3   Well, well, well.

Voice 4   Well, well, well, well.

All   Well, well, well, well, well, well, well.

Pause.

Voice 3   Do you know that Davies is back at fly-half at
the age of thirty-four?

Voice 1   Oggi oggi oggi . . .

All   Oi oi oi . . .

Voice 1   Oggi oggi oggi . . .

All   Oi oi oi . . .

Voice 1   Oggi . . .

All   Oi . . .

Voice 1   Oggi . . .

All   Oi . . .

Voice 1   Oggi oggi oggi . . .

All   Oi oi oi . . .

Fade in music as they all sing along to it drunkenly before leaving the stage to leave **Ace** *alone. Fade in the sound of the sea.*

Ace   And then I saw her. Playing with a yo-yo walking towards the axeman of smalltown. I never knew Marshall had a sister. Mind you, I only knew about Marshall because everyone else did. He was in the papers.

Marshall *sits at the edge of the beach with a fishing rod.* **Bron** *enters with a yo-yo.* **Ace** *observes.*

Marshall   Stop fucking looking at me.

Pause.

Bron   I'm not.

Marshall   You are.

Bron   Who'd look at you?

Marshall   Tart.

Bron   What?

Marshall   Tart is what you are with your yo-yo and face painted and gum.

Bron   Yeh.

Marshall   Yes . . . and what's with the dainty walking.

Bron   Dainty?

Marshall   Yes dainty . . . who do you think you are, the bally?

Bron   That what?

Marshall   The fucking swans on the lake with the tutus and pointy toes . . . I seen them, I've fucking seen them.

Bron   It's ballet, Marsh.

Marshall   Uh?

Bron   Ballet not bally.

Marshall Fuck off, what do you know, fucking tart with the clapping and the dickies and the hoi bastard polloi . . . I seen you.

Bron Seen me what?

Marshall Looking at their balls.

Bron So?

Marshall So I'm your fucking brother.

Bron I didn't know you cared.

Marshall I don't.

Bron So what's the problem?

Marshall There isn't.

Bron Good. Because it's none of your business.

Marshall Fuck off.

Pause.

Bron Caught anything?

Marshall Only crabs, why?

Bron Funny.

Marshall Is it?

Bron Yeh, because you haven't thrown your line in.

Marshall So?

Bron How can you catch any fish if you don't throw your line in?

Marshall Because I'm not fucking interested that's why.

Bron So why do you do it?

Marshall Because it gives me time to think, and it gets me out of that fucking house.

Bron Maybe you should move away.

Marshall To where?

Bron   Anywhere. Make a fresh start.

Marshall   What's the point?

Bron   What's the point staying here? (*Pause.*) Everybody thinking you're a psycho.

Marshall   Shut up. (*Pause.*) I'm not a fucking psycho.

Bron   I don't think the lambs will agree with you.

Marshall   I NEVER FUCKING DID IT ALL RIGHT.

Pause.

Bron   So why did you confess? (*Pause.*) Blame it on Paula Brown. (*Pause.*) If you never did it? (*Pause.*) Marsh?

Marshall   I never did it.

Bron   So who you covering up for? (*Pause.*) Marshall? (*Pause.*) Marshall, answer me.

Marshall   I can't.

Bron   Answer me.

Marshall   I CAN'T RIGHT, I FUCKING CAN'T. (*Pause.*) If you want to know the answer you'll have to ask Bri.

Bron   Bri's gone, Marsh . . .

Marshall   Not for good.

Bron   Two years is a long time.

Marshall   I know it's a long time, but he'll be back, he hasn't gone for ever, I know he'll be back, he's got to come back, Bron, for my sake . . . he's got to tell them the truth.

Pause.

Bron   Tell who the truth, Marsh.

Marshall   Everyone . . . he fucking owes me it, he fucking owes me, Bron. He owes me.

Bron *puts her arm around him.*

Marshall   I never did it, Bron. Everything I did I did
because I fucking loved him. He pulled me out of the river,
he kissed life back into my lungs, he's my brother, my
blood brother. I've got his blood in me and he's got my
blood in him. Why the FUCK DOES HE STILL HATE
ME. WHY, BRON, WHY? (*Pause.*) I only ever said I did it
to win him back. He knows that. SO WHY THE FUCK
DID HE GO AWAY? WHY THE FUCK DID THE
BASTARD HAVE TO GO AWAY?

Ace   Then she saw me. She was beautiful. An apparition.
A fucking angel. I couldn't take my eyes off her. She was a
myth, a fucking fairy from the underworld. I always wanted
to believe in the underworld but I could never find the key,
the door in the rock that would lead me to it. But there it
was in front of me all along. It was just that I couldn't see
it before. Maybe tonight would be the night that the
underworld comes out into the real world and invites it to
dance.

*Fade up music as a whole range of angels, demons and succubae enter
the stage, made up from the voices and dialogue of the earlier park
scene but distorted, made more beautiful, more erotic and more
choreographed.* **Ace** *joins in, as do* **Bron** *and* **Marshall** *in a
wild masque of the underworld which builds to a climax and the
music cuts, freezing the action. Slowly the stage clears leaving an
exhausted* **Ace**.

Ace   Or maybe I was just stoned. I got home and found
dad surrounded in a sea of papers.

Lights up on **Mary Annie** *and* **Manny**.

Manny   Hailstones in Builth Wells the size of golf balls.

Ace *laughs*.

Mary Annie   Uh?

Manny   HAILSTONES, MARY ANNIE, HAILSTONES.

Mary Annie   What's he laughing at?

Ace   Angels and fairies.

Mary Annie   What about them?

Ace   I love them.

Mary Annie   And me (*Pause.*) Where?

Manny   Builth Wells.

Mary Annie   At this time of year?

Manny   Not now, then.

Mary Annie   When?

Manny   1969.

Mary Annie   Uh?

Manny   Hailstones in Builth Wells the size of golf balls.

Mary Annie   What else?

Manny   Wellingtons for sale.

Mary Annie   Wellingtons?

Manny   Green ones. If I had the money then I got now, I'd have bought a pair.

Mary Annie   And corsets?

Manny   Uh?

Mary Annie   Are they selling corsets?

Manny   What you asking me for?

Mary Annie   I need a corset.

Manny   I'm not reading about corsets, I'm reading about golf balls.

Mary Annie   Turn to corsets.

Manny   Mary Annie, mun.

Mary Annie   Go on, see what price they are.

Manny   No.

Mary Annie   Please.

Manny Read it yourself.

Mary Annie I haven't got my glasses.

Manny You don't wear glasses.

Mary Annie I do.

Manny Uh?

Mary Annie It's you that don't wear glasses.

Manny I do, I'm wearing them, only for reading.

Mary Annie They'll be mine.

Manny Uh?

Mary Annie Have a look. (*He takes off his glasses.*) Have you looked?

Manny I'm looking now.

Mary Annie And . . .

Manny Hard to tell.

Mary Annie They're mine.

Manny Haven't got your name on them.

Mary Annie You don't put your name on glasses.

Manny Look like men's glasses to me.

Mary Annie Mine they are.

Manny Like spyglasses.

Mary Annie Spyglasses?

Ace Like *Get Carter* glasses, Mam.

Mary Annie Get who?

Ace Carter, Michael Caine, spies, Russia, wore glasses like those.

Mary Annie Who did?

Ace Michael Caine did.

Mary Annie When?

Manny In the film, mun woman, in the film.

Mary Annie What film?

Manny He just told you, Christ mun Mary Annie, you don't listen to a word nobody says.

Mary Annie Uh?

Manny Not a word.

Mary Annie I'm listening.

Manny Don't know why we bother.

Mary Annie Listen to the listen I am.

Manny We try to explain, but . . .

Mary Annie I'm listening . . . I'M LISTENING . . . Manny?

Manny 1961 . . . 1971 . . . 1981 . . . 1991.

Ace I went upstairs and watched the ants I killed with Floret three days earlier decompose on the windowsill, only bits of silvery wings remained, filtery, nearly see-through. I lit a spliff and went outside. It was hot. I sat in the water trough looking up at the sky. I'd seen what I think is an angel argue with her brother about things I couldn't hear, and I danced with the hobgoblins of fairyland.

Slowly the stage is filled with succubae holding black funereal umbrellas. **Ace** *looks at them, afraid this time as* **Bri** *emerges from under an umbrella pointing an imaginary gun at him.*

Bri Boom . . . Boom . . . fairy fairy . . . dead dead. (*He laughs as the stage clears.*)

Ace Six months later our house fell into the sea, simple as that.

Ace *exits as we hear the sound of an approaching storm.* **Mary Annie** *enters alone.*

Mary Annie Manny? Ace? Manny? Nothing. Blackness.

On my own. Wiff on her own. Full moon and a storm. A
bad storm. The fairies will be out. But we won't be able to
see them. Hidden they'll be, in their garden by the lake.
They've shut the door. The door in the rock; they used to
open it, on a day in May, anybody could go, everyone was
welcome, beautiful it was. Just one day. You could eat,
drink, but you couldn't take anything away with you. One
day somebody stole a flower. Greedy they were. Wanted to
take it home. The fairies were angry. They never opened
the door in the rock again. I can still see the lake but I
can't see the door. (*Pause.*) Funny that. (*Pause.*) Funny and
sad. You've made me sad. I'm crying. You made me cry.
Real tears not tiny tears. I was a summer baby with a
summer memory. Look, here I am crying in my cot.

She hears the sound of a baby crying.

Can you hear me crying? Can you? Still I pick myself up
and give myself a cwtch? Little cwtch for Mary Annie who
you call Wiff in your bed? Come for a cwtch, Mary Annie
fach, come for a cwtch.

She gets out of bed and picks up a wailing doll.

Plastic.

She rips the arms off the baby and it falls to the floor.

Bloody plastic!

*The light by now has faded down just on her. She looks around,
suddenly afraid.*

Gurruga, gurruga, gurruga . . . no bell, no lights, can't
see . . .

*Pause. As she continues to speak, the sound of wind, rain, thunder
and approaching sea builds up.*

Blackness . . . hello? Hello? Manny? (*Pause.*) Rain and wind
and sea. (*Pause.*) Manny? Nothing. Less than nothing.
Blackness. Manny, my husband for thirty years who's
counting but me, no anniversary cards or flowers or
choccies? Hello? Language. Why not? Hiccups and

language and all that good evening. Chocky chocky chocky.
Fuck CHOCKY. KitKat. Flake. Who knows the secret of
the Black Magic box. Me, I'm magic. Where is my son
and husband? My hubby. My lover with shit under his
nails. Cowshit. Horseshit. Chickenshit. Your nails know it
all. Colour. Correct. Constitution. Not right. I can spot a
knackered horse by the quality of shit under your nails.
That cow's for the slaughterhouse, that chicken's laid its last
egg, that turkey is OFF-COLOUR. (*Pause.*) Manny? (*Pause.*)
Man? I was dreaming. About the war. About Linus. (*Pause.*)
He ran the Emporium. The shop. In Abercave. By the
island, was a bakehouse. Grapes he grew. Green grapes.
My brother. Older than me. Cheeky I was. The lamb can
never teach the sheep to graze. That's what he said. To
me. Like a catchphrase. He was the sheep. I was the lamb.
It was a saying he had. He was in the war. He came back
from the war. Don't go out, she said, my mother, it's a
tramp. Ten I was. It wasn't a tramp. It was Linus,
unshaved, demobbed, free, in a suit. She fainted mam did
on the slabs. When she saw him. He bought me a bike,
but there were no lights, or street lights. Gurruga, gurruga,
gurruga I shouted, no bell, no lights, can't see. And I'd ride
into the night. (*Pause.*) I've never been afraid of the night
me. I've sat in the bushes listening to fairies in the dark,
dancing. Fairies and angels. I've given them my teeth. I've
seen doors in rocks that lead to the otherworld. In the
dark. On my bike. The one Linus brought with him back
from the war. (*Pause.*) Gurruga . . . gurruga . . . gurruga . . .
no bell, no lights . . . (*Pause.*) Can't see. But I'm frightened
tonight . . . (*Pause.*) The wind, and the rain and the sea.
(*Pause.*) Manny . . . ? MANNY?

Lights go up on **Manny** *as the cacophony increases. He is soaking
wet.*

Manny   I'm still here, Wiff.

Mary Annie   Where have you been? I'm frightened.

Manny   I've been out.

Mary Annie   In this weather? You must be soaking.

Manny   It's coming, Wiff.

Mary Annie   What is?

Manny   The sea.

Mary Annie   At this time of night.

Manny   I knew it would come at night.

Mary Annie   But we haven't packed.

Manny   There's no time to pack, where's Ace?

Mary Annie   In bed.

Manny   Get him woken up and take what you can outside into the trailer.

Mary Annie   But . . .

Manny   JUST DO IT, MARY ANNIE.

Mary Annie   Mary Annie, Mary Annie, Mary Annie.

Manny   Have you turned off the electric?

Mary Annie   Yes.

Manny   Rounded up the chickens?

Mary Annie   Yes.

Manny   Got Ronty?

Mary Annie   Ronty's in the shed already barking, can't you hear him?

Manny   I hear him now, go and get him, then take Ace, yourself and whatever you can carry to the trailer.

Mary Annie   I'm going, I'm going.

She exits. **Ace** *enters.*

Ace   It's come then.

Manny   It's come.

Ace   You always said it would come at night.

ny We were born in a shrinking land next to a
__m sea, so go and get your mother and put her in the
trailer.

Ace What about you?

Manny I'll make sure everything's all right here then I'll
be with you.

Ace 10–4.

Manny And hurry.

Ace I'm hurrying, I'm hurrying.

Ace *exits.*

Ace (*off*) Mam ... MAM ...

Mary Annie (*off*) I'm coming, I'm coming.

Clap of thunder as the storm increases.

Manny I knew you'd come at night. Black sea. Wild
horses, wind, rain. What made you angry? Not me. Not us.
I always respected you. Me and you were like that once.
Then you had tantrums, Wiff was right when she said the
sea's gone mad, but why take it out on us? We never
walked on you, we always respected you, we've watched
you raging against the rocks, we've seen you shipwreck
boats, but we put it down to a tantrum. Bear with a sore
head. We knew you were moody, but we respected your
moods, we accommodated them, we put up with them, we
lived side by side with them. You let us sail on your back
in the summer, we paddled in the shallows, we watched
you rage against the cold of winter. But we never
complained. We just said it's the sea. The sea being the
sea. We never thought you'd take our house. My father's
house, and his father before that. Why? Wasn't us who put
oil in you, or gassed you or fished you nearly fishless.
We've pissed in you but we never shit in you. I've smoked
on your back but I never threw my filters in there. From
my fags. Tipped ash, yes, but not butts. Not filters and
definitely no cigars. We never threw rubbish in as a family.

Fertilized the land, that's all I did. They told me to do it.
There's some chemicals to make the grass grow greener,
never said it was full of shit. What do I know about water
tables? Uh? Or gas? Or oil? Or big fishing dredging ships?
Or shoals? I don't know. I didn't know. You've got no
right to pick on me. On us. We're innocent. (*Pause.*) We
were like that once. Me and you. But not no more we're
not. You're on the warpath. You want to take over the
world. Make a new development. You'll only be happy
when fish are drinking in here and seals clapping in here.
When fucking dogfish and crabs are the dancing girls in
here. (*Pause.*) But I'll still be here too. In the locker next to
Davy. Growing gills, growing fins, drinking and talking
through bubbles. Remembering. (*Pause.*) The remembering
fish. That's what they'll call me.

Ace (*off*)   Dad ... DAD ... HURRY ... HURRY.

Pause.

Manny   I'm coming ... I'm coming (*Pause.*) So rip down
our house, sea ... do your worst. (*Pause.*) Because you'll
never beat me. (*Pause.*) We'll still be here. (*Pause.*) I'll still be
here. (*Pause.*) I WILL STILL BE HERE!!!

Manny *stands defiant in the rising maelstrom. As it increases in
ferocity we hear* **Mary Annie** *and* **Ace** *shouting for him. Perhaps
the storm noises could also include text and action from the rest of the
cast. Lights fade to nothing on* **Manny** *as the storm and sea build
to a climax. We reach blackout before the storm noise subsides.*

Part Two

Lights up on **Bri** *standing alone.*

Bri Do you know the memory span of a goldfish only lasts one length of an ordinary domestic tank? He swims along happily, gets to the end of the tank, turns round and thinks look at all that space. Then he swims to the other end, turns round and thinks the same again. And again. And again. No past, no future, just the water, the pressure the movement of the gills, the mouth, feeding, swimming, existing, suspended in a void. No memory, nothing. Don't you think that sounds good.

Lights up on **Manny**, **Ace** *and* **Bron** *standing in exactly the same positions as they were at the beginning.*

Manny And?

Ace She said the car belonged to her brother.

Manny Who's her brother?

Bron Brian. Brian James. Do you know him?

Ace No.

Bron He disappeared into thin air two years ago. My mother thinks.

Lights up on **Mati** *and* **Gruff**

Mati He's dead, Gruff.

Gruff Course he's not dead. What's he want to die for?

Mati Because you never loved him.

Gruff Don't talk crap.

Bron She's always loved him. After all, he's her son.

Mati Just like Marshall is.

Gruff I don't want to talk about Marshall.

Mati   But you loved him, Gruff. You loved him more than anything else in your heart. Until he shamed you. (*Pause.*) In front of all the town. That's why you drink in the Ship and Pilot.

Gruff   I don't drink in the Ship and Pilot no more.

Mati   Exactly, because you don't like the junkies coming up to you and saying hey, Gruff, tell us why the angel with the Jaffa Cakes axed new-born lambs to death on the mountains.

Gruff   He's never an angel.

Mati   I know but that's what you called him, you called him an angel in front of Bri, you let him lie on the sitting-room floor with milk and Jaffa Cakes, you taught him to fish, you taught him how to tie flies, purple demons, cochabondees, but you never took Bri. Bri was a fat lazy bastard who couldn't do anything to please you.

Gruff   That's not true, Mati.

Mati   It is true, Gruff, he only did up that car for you and him to go for a ride in. An 1800 TC blue Marina. He only put tinted glass in it so you could go for a drive. Just you and him in the car. Talking chokes, talking fanbelts, talking father-and-son talk in private, behind tinted glass, away from the eyes of the town.

Gruff   No.

Mati   Yes, Gruff, yes, he wanted to win you back and when he'd won you back he could win his brother back, turn back the clock to how it used to be before he fell in that river. A family again. Turned back the time. Started again. But you never let him, he was always second best, it would have been all right if he wanted me, but he knew he already had me. He wanted you and you turned away from him, and you didn't care. You didn't fucking care.

Gruff   Shut up, Mati ... SHUT UP.

Mati   He's dead, Gruff. You killed something in him. And he's never coming back. (*Pause.*) And now you've lost your angel too. (*Pause.*) Because he's shamed you. (*Pause.*) Instead of an angel, you just got a lost boy waiting for his brother to come back. That's why he goes to the airport. But he won't be back. That son's lost for good.

Mati *walks away as the lights change and come up on* **Marshall**, *sitting with his fishing rod staring at the sea.* **Gruff** *approaches.*

Gruff   Caught anything?

Marshall   No.

Gruff   I pished on my hand.

Marshall   Oh.

Gruff   It's them button-up flies, don't know why your mam buys them for me. Too trendy for me. I'm a zip-man. I like a zip. Always have, always will be. (*Pause.*) We haven't been fishing together for a long time.

Marshall   No.

Gruff   We'll have to do it again.

Marshall   Maybe.

Pause.

Gruff   Where you been? (*Pause.*) Marshall?

Marshall   Bonin said he saw him at a football match. On the TV. He said he was a face in the crowd.

Gruff   Where?

Marshall   Chelsea versus Arsenal in the cup.

Gruff   Is that where you been . . . London?

Marshall   No.

Gruff   Oh.

Marshall   There's no point.

Gruff   Why not?

Marshall Because he supported Manchester United, Dad. He fucking hated Arsenal.

Gruff Don't we all. (*Pause.*) So where you been?

Marshall To the airport.

Gruff Heathrow?

Marshall Rhoose. He liked to watch the planes take off and land.

Gruff And take down the numbers?

Marshall No . . . just watch them take off and land.

Gruff He's a funny bugger your brother.

Marshall He used to spend hours there, time would stand still for him there.

Gruff He's always been terrible with time. (*Pause.*) What I mean is . . . if time ran by his clock, trains and planes and buses would crash . . . everywhere.

Marshall Uh?

Gruff Him and time. He's a law to his own.

Marshall Yeh.

Gruff Trains and planes would crash. Because of the time zones. Everybody'd be too scared to take off.

Marshall I don't follow, Dad.

Gruff Well, planes would take off on one side of the world at the same time as another eighty would take off somewhere else in the world.

Marshall So?

Gruff So if they were running on Bri's time, and his time's all over the place, all the time zones would be all over the place too. They'd all meet in the middle and crash, none of them knowing what time it was when it happened.

Marshall   Because they were on Bri's time?

Gruff   Exactly, so Pakistan would be phoning up Australia at the same time that the Poles were phoning up the Argentine asking . . .

Marshall   What happened to our planes?

Gruff   All at the same time, but nobody would know what time it was because all the clocks would be on Bri's time so the only way they could sort it out would be . . .

Marshall   TO PHONE BRI.

Gruff   Exactly.

Marshall   But he'd be out.

Gruff   Yeh.

Marshall   On the razz.

Gruff   On the town.

Marshall   On the nest.

Gruff   And all the while the world would be phoning him to ask him the time.

Marshall   In his room. Man. United clock by his bed ticking away on its own.

Gruff   On Bri time.

Marshall   Bri time.

Gruff   Not any fucking time but . . .

Marshall   Bri time.

Gruff   Phones ringing every second, the world calling.

Marshall   All the dead people.

Gruff   All the living people wanting news.

Marshall   But my brother is out.

Gruff   Out.

Marshall OUT.

Gruff The bastard.

Marshall He should be ashamed of himself. He should be BASTARD ASHAMED.

Gruff Yes.

Marshall The least he could do was buy himself a FUCKING ANSAMACHINE.

Gruff Exactly. WHAT A STUPID TWAT MY SON IS. ALL THIS PAIN BECAUSE OF HIM.

Marshall Pain. Doesn't he know that people still fucking care for him.

Gruff That his father . . .

Marshall And his brother still . . .

Both FUCKING LOVE HIM!

Gruff So why did he fuck off? Why doesn't he keep in touch?

Marshall All he's got to do is to PICK UP THE FUCKING PHONE.

Gruff OR WRITE A LETTER?

Marshall To show that he's alive, but has he?

Gruff No. Because he's a FAT LAZY BASTARD AND I LOVE HIM.

Marshall And me. He pulled me out of the river. HE KISSED AIR INTO MY LUNGS.

Gruff So after two years of nothing, why the FUCK DOESN'T HE RING OR PHONE OR TELL US HE'S ALIVE?

Marshall THE BASTARD.

Gruff THE TWAT.

Marshall I FUCKING HATE HIM.

Gruff   I FUCKING HATE HIM

Light goes up on **Bron** *and* **Mati**.

Bron   I FUCKING HATE HIM.

Mati   I FUCKING HATE HIM.

Gruff   THE WHOLE OF THE ARGENTINE AND
POLAND AND PAKISTAN BASTARD HATE HIM.

Pause.

Marshall   So come back, Bri . . . come back.

Gruff   Come back.

Mati   I love you.

Bron   I love you.

Gruff   I love you.

Mati *and* **Gruff** *exit.*

Bron   But he hasn't come back.

Marshall   And I want him back, Bron. To explain.
(*Pause.*) It wasn't me who killed those lambs, Bron, it was
Bri, I made the Paula Brown story up.

Bron   Why?

Marshall   Because he said. He told me to. He said . . .

Lights up on **Bri**.

Bri   You owe me one. You fucking owe me one, man.

Marshall   But why the fuck did you do it, Bri?

Bri   Why do you think?

Marshall   I wouldn't have asked if I'd known, Bri.

Bri   Can't you work it out for yourself?

Marshall   They were just lambs, Bri, what the fuck have
you got against lambs, Bri?

Bri   Because they just happened to be there, and will you quit putting Bri at the end of all your sentences?

Marshall   Uh . . . ?

Bri   Do you do it to remind yourself of who I am? Do you?

Marshall   No.

Bri   I PULLED YOU OUT OF THAT RIVER YOU FUCK. (*Pause.*) You don't need to put Bri at the end of your sentences. I'm Bri, normal Bri. Normal Norman, the normallest one in all of the town. (*Pause.*) I'm your brother. You aren't an angel, Marsh. You're just my brother. Who I pulled out of the water. (*Pause.*) You were dead. I didn't pull you out so you could grow up and ignore me, man, to put Bri at the end of your sentences. If I'd known you were going to do that I'd have left you on the bank for dead. (*Pause.*) You owe me, Marsh. You fucking owe me.

Bri *exits.*

Marshall   So I took the rap. Made up a story. I took the axe one night, went up the mountains 'til I came to a farm. I saw a woman feed chickens.

Mary Annie *enters throwing feathers in the air as if it was feed.*

Marshall   I waited for her to go inside until it was dark and then . . .

Pause.

Bron   What, Marsh?

Marshall   I fucking murdered them, with Bri's axe. I did it for him.

Ace *screams and brings an axe down hard on a piece of wood.*
Mary Annie *enters holding a dead chicken.*

Ace   Bastards.

Mary Annie   Use these.

Ace   Uh?

Mary Annie   Gloves. Plastic gloves.

Ace   I'll be all right.

Mary Annie   Chickens have germs, Ace. Especially dead ones. Here, take the gloves.

Ace   I'll be finished in a minute.

Mary Annie   Please . . .

Ace *takes the gloves, puts them on..*

Mary Annie   Poor chickens.

Ace   Yeh.

Mary Annie   Never knew what hit them.

Ace   No.

Mary Annie   One minute they're sitting on their eggs, the next minute . . . (*Pause.*) I'd only just fed them too. It's too cruel, Ace . . . too cruel. Why did somebody have to do such a thing. (*Pause.*) What you going to do with them?

Ace   Burn them. And the shed and everything in it. Couple of hours from now, you'll never be able to tell there was ever chickens here.

Mary Annie   I liked the chickens. They were my responsibility. Yours and mine. You grew up feeding the chickens.

Ace   Bit of burnt earth, that's all will be left. Then it will be the end of the chicken story. No one will ever know we ever kept chickens. If anybody asks me ever again about chickens, I'll say I don't know, we never had any. The chicken story will be over.

Mary Annie   So what will our story be?

Ace   We'll make up a story, Mam. Don't worry about that, we'll always have a story.

Ace *lights a Zippo and he and* **Mary Annie** *watch the chicken shed go up in flames.* **Mary Annie** *exits,* **Manny** *enters.*

Bron   I'm sorry, Ace.

Ace   It's not your fault.

Bron   He did it for Bri.

Ace   Yeh.

Bron   I'm sorry.

Ace   Forget it.

Manny   The bastard, the murdering little bastard and there's me thinking . . .

Ace   It's over, Dad, in the past.

Manny   You've changed your tune.

Ace   It's called love, Dad.

Manny   Love?

Ace   Love. I think I'm in love.

Manny   Love, Ace . . . is a mystery.

Ace   Love, Dad . . . is an angel in a blue Marina with leather upholstery.

Crash in Suede's 'White Trash' as the set clears and we join **Ace** *and* **Bron** *in the car. Music plays on the radio. Sound and lights create the sense of movement.*

Ace   Who's this?

Bron   Suede. 'White Trash'.

Ace   I like it.

Bron   Me too. You going to keep all that to yourself or can I have some?

Ace   Here . . . (*He passes her the joint. She smokes.*) What's Bron short for?

Bron   Bronwen.

Ace   What's it mean?

Bron   Pure one. Bron means breast, wen means white, you have to work the rest out.

Pause.

Ace   Bron also means nearly. (*Pause.*) As in bron gorffen.

Bron   Nearly finished.

Ace   Yeh. You speak Welsh?

Bron   Yeh. You?

Ace   Only when I was small. (*Pause.*) I like Welsh.

Bron   Why?

Ace   Because it's got gaps.

Bron   What kind of gaps?

Ace   Like it's not all hard and fast; like there are rules but there are still gaps . . . like to fill in, the meaning . . . you got to work the meaning out for yourself . . . like in English you say 'The cat sat on the mat' . . .

Bron   Yeh . . .

Ace   Well, in Welsh you could say the cat sat in front of the fire . . . you wouldn't have to mention the mat at all. (*Pause.*) What I mean is the cat could be anywhere yet at the same time you know it's on the mat in front of the fire. You got me?

Bron   Think so.

Ace   Like it's got gaps. You make the pictures up in the gaps.

Bron   Like jazz.

Ace   Yeh.

Bron   The difference between jazz and classical music is the gaps.

Ace   If you want, yeh.

Bron   Like an orchestra follows all the notes, give or take how the conductor looks at it.

Ace Yeh.

Bron Whereas in jazz there's a tune but you can get to it however you want, like make up your own notes.

Ace Bingo.

Bron I like gaps.

Ace And me.

Bron I like things I don't understand. Only things I don't understand interest me. Why celebrate what you already know, Ace?

Ace Exactly, Bron.

Bron I mean ... (*She stops the car.*) Toys for Christmas I've already played with should be returned to the shops.

Ace In return for a game you've never seen before but you will never understand.

Bron Exactly.

Ace That's called the fucking thrill of discovery, Bron.

Bron What I don't know I like.

Ace On the button. (*Pause.*) And imagination.

Bron Imagination. Yeh.

Ace A fucking fantasy world.

Bron Yeh. To be Welsh at the end of the twentieth century you got to have imagination, Ace.

Ace Too fucking right.

Bron I mean. The only way to shop in Spar or Tesco's or Safeway's or some shit is not to see Spar or Tesco's at all but imagine something else.

Ace Exactly.

Bron I mean, let's face it who ever said SHOPPING

WAS BEAUTIFUL?

Ace   Not me.

Bron   Nor me.

Lights change to an interior supermarket. **Ace** *and* **Bron** *stand amongst the shoppers.*

Bron   I used to work here.

Ace   Fuck.

Bron   Till two weeks ago.

Ace   Shit.

Bron   I chucked in my job and you know why?

Ace   Why?

Bron   No mystery.

The supervisor **Keith** *enters and watches* **Bron** *eat her lunch.*

Keith   You can tell what kind of a person someone is by the chocolate they eat.

Bron   Is that a fact.

Keith   People who eat Mars bars or Snickers are filling a void in their lives, but those people who eat Turkish Delight like the exotic. (*Takes a Turkish Delight from* **Bron** *and licks it delicately.*) I see that you like the exotic, check-out one.

Bron   Maybe . . . Why?

Keith   Because I've been thinking.

Bron   Really?

Keith   Really. Thinking what an exotic fuck with you would be like.

Bron   Do you think that about every woman you meet, Keith?

Keith   Most women.

Bron   But not all.

Keith No.

Bron What kind of women do you not think about
fucking, Keith?

Keith Old women. Ugly women. My mother. But I'd like
to fuck you. With my hand covered in oil. I'd like to put
my hand on that white cotton blouse of yours. Mark it. Just
on the tit. Unbutton slowly, put my filthy hand on your
lacy white bra. Put my thumb in your mouth. Smudge the
lipstick, then kiss it off. Then fuck you. Till your body's
covered in marks. My marks, my hands. Then lick you. All
of you. Clean. Back to where we started. (*Pause.*) Then I
could talk to you.

Bron Because you'd fucked me.

Keith Yeh ... Talk and talk and fuck and fuck until it
was time to fuck again. Then I'd fuck you again. And
again and again.

Bron Until you couldn't fuck or talk any more?

Keith Yeh.

Pause.

Bron That sounds OK, Keith.

Keith Yeh?

Bron Yeh. Except. We'd have nothing to say. We'd be
sitting in the same room saying nothing. We'd eat and say
nothing. So we'd have to go out, to a bar, to get drunk,
stare at the optics. We'd drink till we couldn't drink no
more. We'd have fucked and fucked and talked and talked
and drunk and drunk till we couldn't talk, drink or fuck
any more.

Keith Uh?

Bron Then we'd go home, Keith, and there you'd be.
Fat and old. Unfuckable. With the TV on. A game show.
Holding a Lottery ticket in your hand and your fingers
crossed. You with your hopes pinned on a sixty-four-
million-to-one chance. And you'd have fuck all to say,

Keith. You'd have frozen in time since the last time we talked. After we fucked. You'd fucked and talked yourself into frozen time. While time all around you was moving on. Then I'd look in the mirror and I'd be as old and ugly as you. Where did it fucking go? All them fucking years. I'd listen to my body decay. I wouldn't be able to move my arms or legs or head. I would only be able to feel my head. It would be heavy, full of the things I dreamt about and never did. I'd feel ashamed. My face would feel as if I'd been skinned. And then I'd scream. I'd scream and scream until I couldn't scream any more. I'd have missed the plot see, Keith, the crack, the dream, the mystery.

Keith   You're fucking weird, check-out one.

Bron   I know and I love it. You want to fuck? Fuck your job and fuck you, Keith. I got a life to live.

She boots him in the groin and as he doubles up she turns to **Ace**.

Bron   I reckon there's a mystery, Ace, do you?

Ace   10–4, Bron, 10–4.

Bron   We just got to use our imagination and stay away from supervisors.

Ace   Yeh.

Bron   Because they fuck up your head, make you forget who you are.

Ace   And so we loaded up the car with booze and fags. We bought a tape and all the while I kept thinking, who are we anyway? Who can we ever be except . . .

Lights go up on **Manny** *and* **Mary Annie** *standing with two suitcases.*

Manny   The sons and daughters of our mothers and fathers.

Ace   Exactly.

Mary Annie   We haven't travelled far, see.

Manny No.

Mary Annie We were born in this house.

Manny I was, and you just down the valley.

Ace Gaerlishe!

Manny Gaerlishe.

Mary Annie Gaerlishe.

Manny This is our land, it grows grass, it grazes sheep.

Mary Annie Do we own grass that graze sheep?

Manny We used to.

Mary Annie But not any more?

Manny No.

Mary Annie The sheep went away.

Manny Yes.

Mary Annie Our fences go unmended.

Manny Yes.

Mary Annie Fence-posts sit in our garden rotting.

Manny We never had a garden.

Mary Annie Not ever?

Manny No.

Mary Annie No border of daffodils, or pansies, or tulip, or rose?

Manny No.

Mary Annie No garden of root vegetables or leeks?

Manny No.

Mary Annie Cabbages?

Manny No.

Mary Annie Peas, sprouts, kidney beans?

Manny None.

Mary Annie Did we keep goats?

Manny No goats ... as such.

Mary Annie Such?

Manny Chickens we kept.

Mary Annie Hooray.

Manny You tended them more than me.

Mary Annie They were my responsibility.

Manny You and the boy's.

Mary Annie Our boy, our boy ... our baby.

Manny Of course our baby. Would we ever dream of asking someone else's baby to tend our chickens?

Mary Annie Not ideally, no.

Manny Exactly. This house has been babied. Gurgles and giggles have been heard here, nappies soiled, back patted and mouth fed. Clothes have been knitted, our baby has been gloved, hatted, even balaclavad, little shoes have gathered dust in our shed.

Mary Annie Little shoes?

Manny Grown out of as he turns into a child. Old shoes discarded in favour of wellingtons and boots.

Mary Annie We should have given them away.

Manny Some we did. Others no doubt you forgot about.

Mary Annie Forgot.

Manny Some things we remember about, others we forget.

Mary Annie Forget.

Manny Not all things can be remembered will, only seated memories are kept in the strongboxes of our minds.

Mary Annie   No standing room.

Manny   No.

Mary Annie   Why's that?

Manny   Because if the standers collide with the sitters and confuse things, memories collide, by the time the bus has reached its destination there is not a clear seated memory to remember.

Mary Annie   How come?

Manny   Because the standers become the sitters and the sitters the standers. The new standers look at the sitters and claim strange memories as their own.

Mary Annie   When they're not.

Manny   No.

Mary Annie   Funny.

Manny   It is.

Mary Annie   Makes you wonder.

Manny   It does.

Mary Annie   How we can still claim some memories as our own?

Manny   It does.

Mary Annie   Struggle to keep an orderly bus as we journey to nowhere.

Manny   Nowhere.

Mary Annie   Place we don't know.

Manny   Exactly.

Mary Annie   You and me.

Manny   Mary Annie and Manny.

Mary Annie   Their house fell into the sea.

Manny   That's why our Ace will have to fly the nest.

Mary Annie   To stay away from the cliffs. STAY AWAY FROM THE CLIFFS WE'LL SHOUT TO HIM.

Manny   And off he'll go.

Mary Annie   Off.

Manny   To other places.

Mary Annie   Cities.

Manny   Towns.

Mary Annie   Countries.

Manny   He'll have to go.

Mary Annie   Mm.

Manny   Not stay here.

Mary Annie   Not after what's happened.

Manny   No.

Mary Annie   I knew the sea had tantrums, but . . .

Manny   What we saw was no tantrum.

Mary Annie   No.

Manny   The sea was on the warpath.

Mary Annie   It was.

Manny   Painted its body blue and marched wild and naked over the land.

Mary Annie   Wanting revenge.

Manny   Revenge.

Mary Annie   For being shit on.

Manny   Shit on.

Mary Annie   From a great height.

Manny   Height.

Mary Annie   Like us.

Manny Us.

Mary Annie Us. Ace. Mary Annie. Manny.

Manny Running for the sun on the flipside of black.

Mary Annie I can see the moon.

Manny Moon.

Mary Annie Moon.

Manny A half moon.

Mary Annie A lit moon.

Manny A half-lit moon.

Mary Annie We can sit on the moon see.

Manny Ride on its back.

Mary Annie Control the sea.

Manny The sea, the sea, the tantrum sea.

Mary Annie We'll make an ally of the sea.

Manny Why not?

Mary Annie Make up and be friends.

Manny Have tantrums with it!

Mary Annie We'll tantrum together!

Manny Us and the sea.

Mary Annie Shitting on the ships of oil and rubbish.

Manny Ships.

Mary Annie Shits!

Manny The governments.

Mary Annie The corporations.

Manny The ugly monied.

Mary Annie Bugger them.

Manny   Exactly.

Mary Annie   Wipe them out like Noah.

Manny   The shitted on against the shitters.

Mary Annie   Then the sea will recede.

Manny   Peaceful.

Mary Annie   We'll mop up the carpets.

Manny   Rebuild the house.

Mary Annie   And start again.

Manny   Cleaned.

Mary Annie   De-lotteried.

Manny   De-governed.

Mary Annie   Ungoverned.

Manny   Free.

Mary Annie   We'll call back our sheep.

Manny   And our chickens.

Mary Annie   And our Ace.

Manny   Grown Ace.

Mary Annie   He'll cross bridges to find us.

Manny   He will.

Mary Annie   We'll have to cook a bird.

Manny   We will.

Mary Annie   In a pot, a big bird.

Manny   Sit around a table.

Mary Annie   And talk.

Manny   We'll have to remember to talk.

Mary Annie   We will.

Manny   Remember what we talked about now.

Mary Annie   Now.

Manny   Start again.

Mary Annie   Mm.

Manny   Get a sheep dog.

Mary Annie   Name him Ronty.

Manny   Remake Ronty.

Mary Annie   Buy what we need and . . .

Manny   Need what we buy.

Mary Annie   Exactly.

Manny   No more. Build 'em high, sell 'em cheap.

Mary Annie   None.

Manny   No more gadgets with no instructions.

Mary Annie   No vacuum cleaners.

Manny   No.

Mary Annie   Or hair dryers.

Manny   No.

Mary Annie   Nothing but a bed.

Manny   A good bed.

Mary Annie   So that we can lie back and look at the moon.

Manny   The half moon.

Mary Annie   The half-lit moon. The moon that don't snore, don't burp and takes your drawers down gently. A moon with long fingers, warm fingers and clean nails.

Manny   Huh!

Mary Annie   To take my drawers down gently! A moon you can hide under the bedclothes and watch it rise in the night. It hasn't risen yet, Manny ... I'm watching.

Manny   I'm too old, Wiff.

Mary Annie   Night-time is the right time.

Manny   I'm sixty-six.

Mary Annie   Only one short of the devil.

Manny   My arteries have hardened.

Mary Annie   Drink more whiskey.

Manny   My bones are brittle.

Mary Annie   Thins the blood.

Manny   My skin is sagging.

Mary Annie   Fire in your belly.

Manny   I'm shrinking.

Mary Annie   I know.

Manny   I swear I've lost two inches.

Mary Annie   What!

Manny   Every year I roll up my trousers, haven't you noticed?

Mary Annie   Size isn't everything, Manny.

Manny   No, Wiff.

Mary Annie   No.

Manny   Turn off the lights then and let me put your moon on my chest.

Mary Annie   Why not.

They kiss then snuggle under the bedclothes. They make love as the whole supermarket starts to dance with shoppers and trolleys, much to **Keith***'s despair.* **Ace** *and* **Bron** *get into the car as the dance ends.*

Ace   Where to?

Bron   THE AIRPORT! WHERE ELSE!

Ace   And I smiled and watched her drive. I didn't care
where. We had the booze, we had the fags, we had the
draw and I'd found a babe. We were stoned and
beautiful taking time out in the country, innocent and free.
And as we drove further and further and higher and higher
into the night I swear I saw most of Wales spread out in
front of me. Like a carpet on an uneven floor. Not even a
floor just an idea of a floor. And the carpet? It wasn't
fucking Axminster that's for sure, but who needed
Axminster when I had all this. I could see for miles. Into
England, Devon, Cornwall and beyond Cornwall, France,
then Spain and right at the bottom at the far end of the
horizon, I swear I can see the lights of North Africa. All of
Europe spead out in front of me, of us. I turned to Bron,
only a silhouette behind the wheel, only the embers of the
joint showing me she was still there.

Bron   I'm still here, Ace.

Ace   I never thought I'd ever see this far, Bron. Maybe
I'm imagining it, my head playing tricks.

Bron   If you can see it, Ace, it's there. Who gives a fuck.

Ace   And she was right. As I sat in the car that night
looking out from the back of beyond to the shores of North
Africa, I felt in my bones that the times are a-changing.
Maybe I can soon call myself a European. A Welsh
European, with my own language and the rudiments of
another on the tip of my tongue, German, French, Spanish,
Portuguese, Russian, Czech, even English. Will speaking a
new language break the chains of a fucked-up head? Will I
be able to be who I want to be then put who I want to be
back in the fucked-up bit so it's not fucked up no more? I
hope so, man. But I ain't the only fucked-up bastard out
there. Everybody's got fucked-up bits. A design flaw that
only some can ever straighten out, phobias, fantasies,
desires, things they don't even know they got locked up in
the strongboxes of their brains. It ain't just me, man. I
know it ain't just me. There's millions of you out there. So
many secrets and so little time. It ain't only me, man, it

ain't only me. (*Pause.*) And then she said . . . right out of the blue . . .

The sound of the car suddenly stops, the sense of movement stops.

Bron Do you think my brother's dead?

Lights up on **Bri**.

Bri For a year and a half I lived in the city where I knew no one and no one knew me. Then I hitched back to that seaside town I used to call home. I checked into a motel in the services on the outskirts of town, the Gas Station Motel, I look in the mirror but it isn't me I see staring back at me. It's him.

Gruff *enters.*

Gruff Don't lie, Bri. Lying will get you nowhere in this world.

Bri Every lamb's neck I snapped was yours. I did it for you, Dad, I did it for you.

He drinks from a bottle and exits as does **Gruff**. **Manny** *enters.*

Ace And I said I don't know, who is your brother. And then she told me her story. But her story reminded me of our story, Dad.

Manny We don't talk about that story any more, Ace. That story is locked up in the strongbox of our minds.

Ace I know that but . . .

Manny That story is our secret, Ace. It's family. It's a family secret.

Ace But . . .

Manny WILL YOU SHUT UP ABOUT OUR FUCKING STORY!

Suddenly there is the sound of a flush. **Mary Annie** *comes out of the toilet and looks at* **Ace** *uncertainly.*

Mary Annie The toilet's spotless. I make sure of that.

Always has been. Single and dual flush. No graffiti. (*Pause.*)
No vandals. (*Pause.*) Done out in blue. (*Pause.*) Fresh coat
not long ago. Sea-blue washbasin with aquamarine finish
and brass pipe fittings. (*Pause.*) Bit dusty but what do you
expect? I'm old. (*Pause.*) Do you know we once won a
holiday to Jamaica? Off the corn flakes? (*Pause.*) But we
never went. (*Pause.*) Are you looking for our son? Is he,
Manny?

Manny No, Wiff.

Mary Annie That's good. Because he's gone out. Do you
know I caught him reading William Shakespeare once? The
Collected Works? Need a magnifying glass to see the
writing. He keeps a diary my son. His name's Hywel.
Hywel Ace. But he's gone out, I'm sorry. (*Pause.*) Do you
know him? (*Pause.*) Mmm?

Ace I am him, Mam.

She looks hard at him. Pause.

Mary Annie Don't be so soft. Do you think I don't
know my own son? Be off with you. You hear me? Be off.

Ace *doesn't move.* **Mary Annie** *looks vulnerable. She walks
towards her bed. Picks up the plastic dolly and pops off its head. She
throws it at him. He doesn't move. She then points an imaginary
shotgun at him.*

Mary Annie Boom . . . boom. (*Pause.*) Dead. Dead.
(*Pause.*) Fairy. Fairy.

She looks at him then exits.

Manny And?

Ace Then we went to the airport.

The sound of aircraft coming in to land fills the whole arena. **Bron**
and **Ace** *sit at the perimeter fence watching the landing plane. The
noise subsides. They drink and smoke spliffs.*

Bron That's a seven four seven.

Ace Yeh?

Bron   Cruising speed 515 miles per hour at an altitude of 33–37,000 feet. (*Pause.*) My brother Bri was into planes. I came with him two days before he went missing. (*Pause.*) It's his car.

Ace   It's a nice car.

Bron   He lost his licence. ·

Ace   That's a drag.

Bron   My mother thinks he's dead.

Ace   What do you think?

Bron   I don't know. Sometimes I think he's alive, other times . . .

Ace   What?

Bron   I don't know . . . something . . . in his eyes . . .

Ace   What, Bron, what?

Lights up on **Bri** *looking dishevelled and wasted. Music plays on the car radio.*

Bri   Spell catastrophe.

Bron   Mm?

Bri   Y or an E?

Bron   E I think.

Bri   You sure?

Bron   Yeh . . . I reckon it's E.

Bri   E . . . C . . . A . . . T . . . A . . . S . . . T . . . R . . . O . . . P . . . H . . . E. (*Pause.*) Means fucking endgame, like when a plane crashes right, they say the PanAm catastrophe.

Bron   I know what it means, Bri.

Bri   Like disaster, only catastrophe's like more disastrous.

Bron   Like catastrophic, you mean.

Bri   Bingo. (*Pause.*) Quantas is the airline, see.

Bron   Uh?

Bri   No crashes in its history, fucking catastropheeless.

Bron   Who are they?

Bri   Australian, never had a crash.

Bron   Gunn might have flown with them. Is he still out there? Australia?

Bri   As far as I know. (*Pause.*) Who's this?

Bron   Marc Bolan.

Bri   Who's he?

Bron   T. Rex ... 'Metal Guru' ... seventies band, don't you know anything, Bri?

Bri   Oh.

Bron   Smashed into a tree in Putney he did ... in his Mini. They have vigils there on his anniversary.

Bri   Like light candles and sing songs?

Bron   Something like that.

Bri   Wonder if people will do that for me?

Bron   You got to have done something to do that.

Bri   Like what?

Bron   Like something. Be in a band or something.

Bri   I suppose. (*Pause.*) Or disappear.

Bron   What you want to disappear for?

Bri   I didn't. (*Pause.*) I just said it was an option.

Bron   Some option.

Pause.

Bri   Come on, let's go home.

Bron   Haven't finished our cans.

Bri   We'll drink them on the way.

Bron   They'll catch you one day, Bri, and then you'll be fucked. No more driving.

Bri   So then fucked I'll be. Come on. I'll race you to the car.

Bri *exits. Lights come back up on* **Ace** *and* **Bron**.

Bron   Two days after that they arrested him and BOOM. (*Pause.*) We haven't seen him since.

Ace   Maybe he's gone underground.

Bron   Uh?

Ace   Found a door in a rock one day and now he's dancing with the fucking hobgoblins of fairyland.

Bron   If only.

Ace   It's the underworld see, Bron, the fucking otherworld dancing . . . that's where he'll be. Every now and then, they come up from other underworld and into this world.

Bron   Come off it.

Ace   I've seen them, Bron. I danced with them. But they don't come up too often any more because we do bad things to them.

Bron   What kind of bad things? (**Ace** *looks away*.) Ace?

Ace   They say we'll take you to a place so beautiful that your brain explodes, you can drink, eat, fuck do whatever but you can't take anything back with you or you'll never be able to come again; but what happens?

Bron   We try to take something back?

Ace   On the button, we try and take a souvenir, a memento of where we've been, thinking they won't notice and then bingo, we fall unconscious on the ground, and when we wake up that memento has disappeared and we're standing in a field in the middle of nowhere thinking where the fuck am I? Who the fuck am I and where the fuck am

I going?

Bron And?

Ace And then you spend the whole of the rest of your life trying to go back to that world, Bron, trying to find the key to the door, trying to find the fucking door itself, but you won't, man, because you fucked it all up. You had your chance. One chance you get, Bron . . . and you blow it.

Bron That's heavy, Ace.

Ace It is heavy, that's why you don't see the otherworld no more, Bron. Cos they're pissed off with us, they're not going to give us any more throws because we don't know how to handle a good time when it's staring us right in the face. The underground parties from now on, Bron, are strictly members only.

Bron Apart from Brian James.

Ace Apart from Brian James, yeh.

Bron Cos Brian James can handle a good time.

Ace Yeh.

Bron He's not going to want to bring souvenirs back with him because he's got it all photographed in his head.

Ace Yeh.

Bron So he won't come back because he's having too good a time, you mean?

Ace Yeh.

Bron And time down there don't mean the same.

Ace No, like a year for us is only a minute to them.

Bron Or less.

Ace Yeh.

Bron In that case Bri's only been missing for two minutes so what's the point in worrying?

Ace Exactly. (*Pause.*) I thought you were an angel from the otherworld when I first saw you, Bron.

Bron I'm no angel.

Ace I dreamt that I danced with you underground. I saw you dance then you came up to me and said . . .

Bron Would you like to come to a hotel with me and make love until the dark turns to orange?

Lights change, and come up on **Manny**.

Manny And . . .

Ace I said I'd love to.

Manny And?

Ace We went, Dad. To the Gas Station Motel on the outskirts of the town where she danced for me and I danced for her.

Lights change to a motel room. **Bron** *and* **Ace** *enter, they undress, hungrily tearing at clothes and body, the rest of the cast may join in in this dance of sex – wrapping sheets, twisting bodies and generally creating erotic mayhem – the dance comes to a climax. Lights change and come up on* **Ace** *standing in the dawn light, dressed only in jeans.* **Bron** *joins him at the window.*

Manny And then?

Ace I said . . .

Manny What? (*Pause.*) What, Ace, WHAT?

Ace Can you keep a secret, Bron?

Bron Try me.

Ace Like a real dark secret . . .

Bron Course I can, Ace . . . say.

Pause.

Manny Tell me, Ace, tell me!

Bron Ace?

Ace   We saw an angel once.

Manny   You stupid bastard.

Ace   Me and my father.

Manny   How could you?

Bron   When?

Ace   In the middle of the night.

Manny   Jesus.

Ace   I woke up, I heard someone outside.

Manny   FOR CHRIST SAKE, ACE, IT'S A FAMILY SECRET!

Lights change. **Bron** *exits to the shadows.* **Ace** *enters dragging a body.* **Manny** *enters wearing pyjamas underneath his undercoat.*

Manny   WHAT THE HELL ARE YOU DOING?

Ace (*dragging body*)   Give me a hand, Dad.

Manny   It's the middle of the night!

Ace   I got a bloke here . . . I heard him snooping outside. I caught him red-handed. Give me a hand.

Manny   Snooping?

Ace   Yeh. Help me drag him in.

They drag the body to the middle of the room.

Manny   Have you killed him?

Ace   Course I haven't killed him, just knocked him out.

Manny   Good boy.

Ace   Is it safe to leave him here??

Manny   Uh?

Ace   'Til he comes round?

Manny   Who is he?

Ace   What you think?

Manny   Do I know him?

Ace   Maybe we should put a blanket over him.

Manny   Uh?

Ace   'Til he comes round.

Manny   You going to leave him there?

Ace   Where else shall I put him?

Manny   He'll be in the way there.

Ace   That's what I was asking.

Manny   Uh?

Ace   I just asked you if I should leave him here, I just asked, Dad, and you didn't say nothing.

Manny   You can't leave him there.

Ace   That's what I said.

Manny   Somebody's bound to fall over him. You mam will fall over him when she comes downstairs.

Ace   That's what I was saying.

Manny   You got to move him from there or he'll cause an accident.

Ace   Where shall I put him then?

Manny   Put him up against the wall.

Ace   Will he be safe there?

Manny   Safer than he is now, he's right in the middle there, he could cause an accident, people cross there all the time, this is a busy room.

Ace   I'm not putting him upstairs.

Manny   Uh?

Ace   Upstairs, he's not going upstairs, I got stuff upstairs.

Manny   He'll freeze in the shed.

Ace   I'll put a heater in there, a gas heater with settings, controllable settings, keeps it cosy.

Manny   A heater?

Ace   A controllable one, you can put it on setting one for one portion of the fire to come on or two and then full blast is three.

Manny   We could do with something like that in here.

Ace   We can't have it in here.

Manny   Uh?

Ace   Mam don't like gas.

Manny   Uh?

Ace   That's what she said, afraid it'll blow up, she said gas is dangerous.

Manny   Blow up?

Ace   Yeh.

Manny   In here?

Ace   Yeh.

Manny   Gas?

Ace   Yeh.

Manny   Controllable gas?

Ace   That's what I said, I said it won't blow up, Mam, cos it's controllable, but she wouldn't have it. She said it was gas, natural gas, she said you can't control it because it's natural.

Manny   Natural?

Ace   That's what she said.

Manny   It's not natural.

Ace   Uh?

Manny   It comes in a bottle.

Ace   I told her that but she still said it was natural, and what's natural is wild, wild means it can't be controlled, if it can't be controlled, it's liable to be unstable, if it's unstable it's liable to blow up at any time.

Manny   But you said you've got controls on it.

Ace   I have.

Manny   So what she talking about?

Ace   That's why I put it in the shed.

Manny   Uh?

Ace   Because she wouldn't have it.

Manny   It's handy.

Ace   It is ... Handygas it's called.

Manny   Well, there we are then, they wouldn't call it handy if it was wild, it would be against the law, they'd put a stop to it, the advertising people. (*Pause.*) Did you follow all the instructions?

Ace   It's on the lid. It's permanent. Every time you turn it on you have to lift the lid, the instructions are on the lid, right in front of you, can't miss them.

Manny   That's good.

Ace   Keeps it cosy in there.

Manny   I'll have a word with her.

Ace   That's why I don't want to put him in there.

Manny   Uh?

Ace   Because he'll snoop around. I got everything all in order there.

Manny   What you got in there?

Ace   It's all in order.

Manny That's good.

Ace I don't want him snooping around in there.

Manny No.

Ace I got a lot of stuff in there, all broken down into compartments, diaries labelled so that I can get to things without having to pull all the drawers and stuff out.

Manny You haven't thrown nothing out?

Ace No.

Manny Because you'll want it one day.

Ace Mmm.

Manny It's your stuff.

Ace Mm.

Manny You'll need it one day too . . . you listening?

Ace I'm listening. (**Ace** *starts to drag the body into the corner.*) What you reckon?

Manny He's better there, better there than where he was, he could have caused an accident, he's safe over there, out of harm's way.

Ace Yeh.

Manny Let's have a look at him.

He looks.

Ace Do you know him?

Manny No. You?

Ace I don't know.

Manny Uh?

Ace I seen him somewhere.

Manny Where?

Ace Don't know, his face has got something about it.

Manny   I can't place him.

Ace   I don't know him. (*Pause.*) Prowling he was see. Snooping about.

Ace   You said.

Ace   I had to hit him.

Manny   Mm.

Ace   Didn't mean to hurt him, not permanent, just like knock him out, teach him a lesson.

Manny   Mm.

Ace   He was after the chickens he was, Dad.

Manny   How do you work that out?

Ace   He was by the chicken shed when I hit him.

Manny   He could be from the council.

Ace   No.

Manny   Could be.

Ace   He hasn't got a tie on.

Manny   Uh?

Ace   No tie, no suit, can't be from the council, all the council wear suits on official business, like council business, I seen them.

Manny   Maybe he's not from the council then.

Ace   Maybe he isn't.

Manny   Mind you.

Ace   What?

Manny   Well, they don't all wear ties these days.

Ace   Uh?

Manny   I seen a few of them walking round, the hoi polloi without ties or suits.

Ace   Where?

Manny   In the village, walking about.

Ace   Are you sure they're on the council?

Manny   Positive, whatsisname Watkins, he's the bugger who said our house is unstable.

Ace   The bastard.

The body makes a noise. **Ace** *smacks him. The body goes unconscious again.*

Manny   What you do that for?

Ace   I don't know.

Manny   He was coming round.

Ace   I know ... but ...

Manny   You should have let him come round.

Ace   I wasn't ready, Dad.

Manny   Uh?

Ace   We haven't worked out what we're going to do with him yet.

Manny   What's to work out?

Ace   We can't just leave him go.

Manny   Why not, can't we?

Ace   Because he'll go to the police.

Manny   So?

Ace   He'll tell them we hit him, then we'll have the council and the police on us.

Manny   But he was stealing our chickens.

Ace   We haven't got no chickens.

Manny   I know, but he don't know that and you said you saw him going towards the chicken shed.

Ace   He was.

Manny   To steal chickens?

Ace   We haven't got none, Dad, they're all dead.

Manny   So what you want to hit him for?

Ace   Because I thought he was from the council, I thought he'd come to knock down our house.

Manny   But he hasn't got a tie!

Ace   Not all the COUNCILLORS WEAR TIES, DAD.

Manny   So why did you hit him, Ace?

Ace   I don't know, I said.

Manny   WHY DID YOU HIT HIM, ACE?

Ace   I DON'T FUCKING KNOW ALL RIGHT. I SAW HIM OUT THERE PROWLING AROUND, I PICKED UP THE FENCE-POST AND HIT HIM. (*Pause.*) That's all there is to it. (*Pause.*) I saw him going towards the chickens, I knew we didn't have any no more, but he didn't. He was walking towards the shed. Chickens he was after, or eggs. He had that look about him. Like the look of a thief. Shifty he was. Look at his face. Don't he look shifty to you?

Manny   He's out cold.

Ace   Yeh, but shifty and out cold.

Manny   A bit.

Ace   He's shifty, Dad, there's no two ways about it. He's got the face of a thief. A chicken stealer, an egg stealer. That's why I hit him.

Manny   With a fence-post.

Ace   Yeh.

Manny   The ones you're going to build a fence with?

Ace   Yes.

Manny   The ones that have been sitting out there since they came.

Ace   Two hands I got, Dad.

Manny   Two winters they been out there.

Ace   My responsibility was to the chickens, anyway you were going to help me.

Manny   I'm too old, Ace.

Ace   I can't do everything, Dad.

Manny   Too old and fucked.

Ace   You're not fucked.

Manny   I am.

Ace   You're not . . . I NEEDED A HELPING HAND, DAD.

The body moves. **Ace** *moves to hit him.* **Manny** *holds him back.*

Manny   No . . . don't.

Ace   But . . .

Manny   No let him come round. Then we'll decide what to do with him.

They watch the body move obviously in pain. They watch as he gets to his knees. He looks up at them and pulls down his hood. It is **Bri**. *His face is bloodied but it is unmistakably* **Bri**; *unshaven, confused, bedraggled: as if he's slept under the stars for months. He looks at them.*

Manny   Are you from the council?

But before he can answer, a shot rings out from a double-barrelled shotgun and **Bri** *falls dead and bleeding on the floor.* **Mary Annie** *enters holding a gun.*

Ace   Mam?

Manny   Mary Annie?

Ace *runs to the dead body.*

Ace He's dead.

Mary Annie He's from the otherworld. (*Pause.*) He's come to take our house. (*Pause.*) He's in cahoots with the sea. (*Pause.*) It's not the council we got to be afraid of . . . it's the sea. I seen him watching the house. Talking fairy talk. To himself. Gibberish. Fairy talk. Nonsense. Shouting in the top field. It's where the fairies used to dance until you ploughed the field, Manny. I told you they'd be angry. They put a spell on this house because they couldn't come out and dance no more. In cahoots with the sea. (*Pause.*) Spiteful I call it. We only got a handful of fields. They got fields all over the world. We only ploughed one. But that made them spiteful. They won't be satisfied 'til the house falls into the sea. And us with it. We'll be down there with Seithennin the drunk and Davy Jones in Cantre'r Gwaelod. (*Pause.*) He's a messenger see. Come to give us a warning. It was him that killed the chickens see. Must be. But we got him. It's not the council and their bulldozers we got to be afraid of, it's the fairies. I warned you, Mansell. Don't go ploughing the field but you wouldn't have it. (*Pause.*) I seen them dancing there. When I was out on Linus's bike in the war. I'm not afraid of them. Because I've seen them. I've seen them . . . (*Pause.*) Gurruga . . . gurruga . . . gurruga . . . (*Pause.*) No bell . . . no lights . . . can't see . . . He's a fairy. (*Pause.*) From the underworld. Telling us to get out. But we're not getting out. We're staying. (*Pause.*) We're staying. We're staying. WE WILL STILL BE HERE! (*Pause.*) Good night.

Mary Annie *exits.*

Ace And then we buried him. In the black earth next to the chickens. (*Pause.*) Hoping nobody would notice. (*Pause.*) And they didn't. (*Pause.*) Still didn't stop the house from falling into the sea. (*Pause.*) An angel.

Music as **Bri** *stands, looks at them then walks away.*

Manny And you told her. (*Pause.*) You told her our secret? (*Pause.*) Ace? (*Pause.*) ACE?

Bron *enters.*

Ace We saw an angel once.

Bron When?

Ace In the middle of the night. I woke up, I heard someone outside.

Bron And?

Ace I must have scared him away.

Bron What did he look like?

Ace He wore a tie and a suit, he looked as if he came from the council.

Bron No wings.

Ace None.

Bron No halo.

Ace No.

Bron No wand.

Ace No.

Bron So what makes you think he was an angel? Ace?

Ace My imagination. Only my imagination. To be Welsh at the end of the twentieth century we got to have imagination.

Bron We do.

Ace As you said.

Bron I did.

Ace In your blue Marina.

Bron Yep.

Ace With tinted glass.

Bron With tinted glass.

Ace That we drove into the heart of Saturday night.

Bron   Yes.

Ace   That once belonged to your brother.

Pause.

Bron   My brother's still dancing, Ace. Dancing with the hobgoblins of fairyland.

Ace   Yes.

Bron   He'll come back when he's tired.

Ace   Yeh.

Bron   When the party's over.

Ace   Yeh.

There is a knock on the door. A maid stands there with a cleaning trolley.

Maid   Room service.

Bron   What time is it?

Maid   Twenty to twelve.

Bron   What day?

Maid   Sunday. Check out time's half ten.

Bron   Sorry.

Maid   So I'd appreciate it if you'd hurry up.

Bron   No problem, give us a few minutes.

Maid   Otherwise you'll have to pay extra.

Bron   Two minutes and we're out.

Maid   Two minutes.

Bron   Two minutes.

Maid   I'll be counting.

She exits.

Bron   What's two minutes or two years to a hobgoblin of fairyland?

Ace What's . . .

Bron Exactly. Let's go, Ace.

Ace Let's go.

Manny So you never told her.

Ace No.

Manny Because that's our secret, Ace.

Ace I know, Dad.

Manny It's a family secret we keep in the strongboxes of our minds, Ace.

Ace I know.

Manny We've locked the door and thrown away the key. (*Pause.*) We'll never look in there again will we, Ace?

Ace No, Dad.

Manny Good boy.

Pause.

Ace But at least we know now.

Manny Know what?

Ace That it wasn't an angel.

Manny We've always known, Ace, always. (*Pause.*) There are no angels and no fairies.

Ace Only brothers.

Manny Yes.

Ace And sons.

Manny Yes.

Ace Missing sons of mothers and fathers.

Manny Yes.

Ace Gone mad. (*Pause.*) It was Bri, Dad. It was Bri.

Bron And so we drove home. We didn't say much. We were stoned and beautiful. Ace was my Clyde and I was his Bonnie. I dropped him off at the foot of the mountain. He said . . .

Ace Can I see you again?

Bron Why not. Give me a call.

Ace I will.

Bron Here's my mobile number. It takes messages.

Ace Thanks. I'll ring you.

Bron You do that.

Ace So long, Bron.

Bron So long, Ace.

Ace Then she drove away.

Manny And?

Ace Then I came home.

Pause.

Manny Is that your story?

Ace It is . . . it's the end of my story.

Manny So far.

Ace Yes. (*Pause.*) Did he have a tattoo?

Manny What tattoo?

Ace On his arm. Bron said he supported Manchester United.

Manny Yes.

Ace You looked?

Manny I looked yes.

Ace Oh.

Manny And above it is the word 'mam'.

Ace   Mam.

Manny   And on his shoulder he's got a car.

Ace   What car?

Manny   A blue Marina . . . what else?

Ace   Obviously.

Manny   Obviously.

Ace   The blue Marina 1800 TC.

Manny   Something like that.

Ace   Right.

Pause.

Manny   So put the kettle on instead.

Ace   Yeh.

Manny   So we'll have a cup of tea.

Ace   Right.

Manny   With milk.

Ace   Yeh.

Manny   And sugar.

Ace   Right.

Manny   Well, go on then.

Ace   I'm going, I'm going.

Pause. The two men stand in silence.

Manny   You going or what?

Ace   I'm going, I'm going.

Pause.

Manny   Sons . . . huh. (*Pause.*) Huh . . .

Fade in the sound of the sea. Fade to black.

A SELECTED LIST OF
METHUEN MODERN PLAYS

☐	CLOSER	Patrick Marber	£6.99
☐	THE BEAUTY QUEEN OF LEENANE	Martin McDonagh	£6.99
☐	A SKULL IN CONNEMARA	Martin McDonagh	£6.99
☐	THE LONESOME WEST	Martin McDonagh	£6.99
☐	THE CRIPPLE OF INISHMAAN	Martin McDonagh	£6.99
☐	THE STEWARD OF CHRISTENDOM	Sebastian Barry	£6.99
☐	SHOPPING AND F***ING	Mark Ravenhill	£6.99
☐	FAUST (FAUST IS DEAD)	Mark Ravenhill	£5.99
☐	POLYGRAPH	Robert Lepage and Marie Brassard	£6.99
☐	BEAUTIFUL THING	Jonathan Harvey	£6.99
☐	MEMORY OF WATER & FIVE KINDS OF SILENCE	Shelagh Stephenson	£7.99
☐	WISHBONES	Lucinda Coxon	£6.99
☐	BONDAGERS & THE STRAW CHAIR	Sue Glover	£9.99
☐	SOME VOICES & PALE HORSE	Joe Penhall	£7.99
☐	KNIVES IN HENS	David Harrower	£6.99
☐	BOYS' LIFE & SEARCH AND DESTROY	Howard Korder	£8.99
☐	THE LIGHTS	Howard Korder	£6.99
☐	SERVING IT UP & A WEEK WITH TONY	David Eldridge	£8.99
☐	INSIDE TRADING	Malcolm Bradbury	£6.99
☐	MASTERCLASS	Terrence McNally	£5.99
☐	EUROPE & THE ARCHITECT	David Grieg	£7.99
☐	BLUE MURDER	Peter Nichols	£6.99
☐	BLASTED & PHAEDRA'S LOVE	Sarah Kane	£7.99

- All Methuen Drama books are available through mail order or from your local bookshop.

Please send cheque/eurocheque/postal order (sterling only) Access, Visa, Mastercard, Diners Card, Switch or Amex.

Expiry Date: _____ Signature: _____

Please allow 75 pence per book for post and packing U.K.
Overseas customers please allow £1.00 per copy for post and packing.

ALL ORDERS TO:

Methuen Books, Books by Post, TBS Limited, The Book Service, Colchester Road, Frating Green, Colchester, Essex CO7 7DW.

NAME: _____

ADDRESS: _____

_____

_____

Please allow 28 days for delivery. Please tick box if you do not
wish to receive any additional information   ☐

Prices and availability subject to change without notice.

METHUEN CLASSICAL GREEK DRAMATISTS

☐ AESCHYLUS PLAYS: I (*Persians, Prometheus Bound,*
   Suppliants, Seven Against Thebes)   £9.99
☐ AESCHYLUS PLAYS: II (*Oresteia: Agamemnon, Libation-*
   Bearers, Eumenides)   £9.99
☐ SOPHOCLES PLAYS: I (*Oedipus the King, Oedipus at Colonus,*
   Antigone)   £9.99
☐ SOPHOCLES PLAYS: II (*Ajax, Women of Trachis, Electra,*
   Philoctetes)   £9.99
☐ EURIPIDES PLAYS: I (*Medea, The Phoenician Women, Bacchae*)   £9.99
☐ EURIPIDES PLAYS: II (*Hecuba, The Women of Troy, Iphigenia*
   at Aulis, Cyclops)   £9.99
☐ EURIPIDES PLAYS: III (*Alkestis, Helen, Ion*)   £9.99
☐ EURIPIDES PLAYS: IV (*Elektra, Orestes, Iphigeneia in Tauris*)   £9.99
☐ EURIPIDES PLAYS: V (*Andromache, Herakles' Children,*
   Herakles)   £9.99
☐ EURIPIDES PLAYS: VI (*Hippolytos Suppliants, Rhesos*)   £9.99
☐ ARISTOPHANES PLAYS: I (*Acharnians, Knights, Peace,*
   Lysistrata)   £9.99
☐ ARISTOPHANES PLAYS: II (*Wasps, Clouds, Birds, Festival*
   Time, Frogs)   £9.99
☐ ARISTOPHANES & MENANDER: NEW COMEDY
   (Aristophanes: *Women in Power, Wealth*
   Menander: *The Malcontent, The Woman from Samos*)   £9.99

• All Methuen Drama books are available through mail order or from your local bookshop.

Please send cheque/eurocheque/postal order (sterling only) Access, Visa, Mastercard, Diners Card, Switch or Amex.

☐☐☐☐☐☐☐☐☐☐☐☐☐☐☐☐

Expiry Date:_____ Signature: _____

Please allow 75 pence per book for post and packing U.K.
Overseas customers please allow £1.00 per copy for post and packing.

ALL ORDERS TO:

Methuen Books, Books by Post, TBS Limited, The Book Service, Colchester Road, Frating Green, Colchester, Essex CO7 7DW.

NAME: _____

ADDRESS: _____

_____

_____

Please allow 28 days for delivery. Please tick box if you do not
wish to receive any additional information   ☐

Prices and availability subject to change without notice.

METHUEN STUDENT EDITIONS

☐ SERJEANT MUSGRAVE'S DANCE	John Arden	£6.99
☐ CONFUSIONS	Alan Ayckbourn	£5.99
☐ THE ROVER	Aphra Behn	£5.99
☐ LEAR	Edward Bond	£6.99
☐ THE CAUCASIAN CHALK CIRCLE	Bertolt Brecht	£6.99
☐ MOTHER COURAGE AND HER CHILDREN	Bertolt Brecht	£6.99
☐ THE CHERRY ORCHARD	Anton Chekhov	£5.99
☐ TOP GIRLS	Caryl Churchill	£6.99
☐ A TASTE OF HONEY	Shelagh Delaney	£6.99
☐ STRIFE	John Galsworthy	£5.99
☐ ACROSS OKA	Robert Holman	£5.99
☐ A DOLL'S HOUSE	Henrik Ibsen	£5.99
☐ MY MOTHER SAID I NEVER SHOULD	Charlotte Keatley	£6.99
☐ DREAMS OF ANNE FRANK	Bernard Kops	£5.99
☐ BLOOD WEDDING	Federico Lorca	£5.99
☐ THE MALCONTENT	John Marston	£5.99
☐ BLOOD BROTHERS	Willy Russell	£6.99
☐ DEATH AND THE KING'S HORSEMAN	Wole Soyinka	£6.99
☐ THE PLAYBOY OF THE WESTERN WORLD	J.M. Synge	£5.99
☐ OUR COUNTRY'S GOOD	Timberlake Wertenbaker	£6.99
☐ THE IMPORTANCE OF BEING EARNEST	Oscar Wilde	£5.99
☐ A STREETCAR NAMED DESIRE	Tennessee Williams	£5.99

• All Methuen Drama books are available through mail order or from your local bookshop.

Please send cheque/eurocheque/postal order (sterling only) Access, Visa, Mastercard, Diners Card, Switch or Amex.

☐☐☐☐☐☐☐☐☐☐☐☐☐☐☐☐

Expiry Date:_____Signature: _____

Please allow 75 pence per book for post and packing U.K.
Overseas customers please allow £1.00 per copy for post and packing.

ALL ORDERS TO:

Methuen Books, Books by Post, TBS Limited, The Book Service, Colchester Road, Frating Green, Colchester, Essex CO7 7DW.

NAME: _____

ADDRESS: _____

_____

_____

Please allow 28 days for delivery. Please tick box if you do not
wish to receive any additional information   ☐

Prices and availability subject to change without notice.

METHUEN SCREENPLAYS

☐ BEAUTIFUL THING	Jonathan Harvey	£6.99
☐ THE ENGLISH PATIENT	Anthony Minghella	£7.99
☐ THE CRUCIBLE	Arthur Miller	£6.99
☐ THE WIND IN THE WILLOWS	Terry Jones	£7.99
☐ PERSUASION	Jane Austen, adapted by Nick Dear	£6.99
☐ TWELFTH NIGHT	Shakespeare, adapted by Trevor Nunn	£7.99
☐ THE KRAYS	Philip Ridley	£7.99
☐ THE AMERICAN DREAMS (THE REFLECTING SKIN & THE PASSION OF DARKLY NOON)	Philip Ridley	£8.99
☐ MRS BROWN	Jeremy Brock	£7.99
☐ THE GAMBLER	Dostoyevsky, adapted by Nick Dear	£7.99
☐ TROJAN EDDIE	Billy Roche	£7.99
☐ THE WINGS OF THE DOVE	Hossein Amini	£7.99
☐ THE ACID HOUSE TRILOGY	Irvine Welsh	£8.99
☐ THE LONG GOOD FRIDAY	Barrie Keeffe	£6.99
☐ SLING BLADE	Billy Bob Thornton	£7.99

• All Methuen Drama books are available through mail order or from your local bookshop.

Please send cheque/eurocheque/postal order (sterling only) Access, Visa, Mastercard, Diners Card, Switch or Amex.

☐☐☐☐☐☐☐☐☐☐☐☐☐☐☐☐

Expiry Date:_____ Signature: _____

Please allow 75 pence per book for post and packing U.K.
Overseas customers please allow £1.00 per copy for post and packing.

ALL ORDERS TO:

Methuen Books, Books by Post, TBS Limited, The Book Service, Colchester Road, Frating Green, Colchester, Essex CO7 7DW.

NAME: _____

ADDRESS: _____

_____

_____

Please allow 28 days for delivery. Please tick box if you do not wish to receive any additional information ☐

Prices and availability subject to change without notice.

METHUEN DRAMA
MONOLOGUE & SCENE BOOKS

☐ CONTEMPORARY SCENES FOR ACTORS (MEN)	Earley and Keil	£8.99
☐ CONTEMPORARY SCENES FOR ACTORS (WOMEN)	Earley and Keil	£8.99
☐ THE CLASSICAL MONOLOGUE (MEN)	Earley and Keil	£7.99
☐ THE CLASSICAL MONOLOGUE (WOMEN)	Earley and Keil	£7.99
☐ THE CONTEMPORARY MONOLOGUE (MEN)	Earley and Keil	£7.99
☐ THE CONTEMPORARY MONOLOGUE (WOMEN)	Earley and Keil	£7.99
☐ THE MODERN MONOLOGUE (MEN)	Earley and Keil	£7.99
☐ THE MODERN MONOLOGUE (WOMEN)	Earley and Keil	£7.99
☐ THE METHUEN AUDITION BOOK FOR MEN	Annika Bluhm	£6.99
☐ THE METHUEN AUDITION BOOK FOR WOMEN	Annika Bluhm	£6.99
☐ THE METHUEN AUDITION BOOK FOR YOUNG ACTORS	Anne Harvey	£6.99
☐ THE METHUEN BOOK OF DUOLOGUES FOR YOUNG ACTORS	Anne Harvey	£6.99

• All Methuen Drama books are available through mail order or from your local bookshop.

Please send cheque/eurocheque/postal order (sterling only) Access, Visa, Mastercard, Diners Card, Switch or Amex.

☐☐☐☐☐☐☐☐☐☐☐☐☐☐☐

Expiry Date:_____ Signature: _____

Please allow 75 pence per book for post and packing U.K.
Overseas customers please allow £1.00 per copy for post and packing.

ALL ORDERS TO:

Methuen Books, Books by Post, TBS Limited, The Book Service, Colchester Road, Frating Green, Colchester, Essex CO7 7DW.

NAME: _____

ADDRESS: _____

_____

Please allow 28 days for delivery. Please tick box if you do not
wish to receive any additional information   ☐

Prices and availability subject to change without notice.

METHUEN DRAMA
BERTOLT BRECHT PLAYS

WORLD CLASSICS

☐ COLLECTED PLAYS: ONE (*Baal, Drums in the Night,*
   In the Jungle of Cities, The Life of Edward II of England
   and five one-act plays)   £9.99

☐ COLLECTED PLAYS: TWO (*Man equals Man, The Elephant Calf,*
   The Threepenny Opera, The Rise and Fall of the City of
   Mahagonny, The Seven Deadly Sins)   £9.99

☐ COLLECTED PLAYS: THREE (*St Joan of the Stockyards,*
   Lindbergh's Flight, The Baden-Baden Lesson on Consent,
   He Said Yes/He Said No, The Decision, The Exception and
   the Rule, The Horatians and the Curiatians, The Mother)   £10.99

☐ COLLECTED PLAYS: FIVE (*Life of Galileo, Mother Courage*
   and her Children)   £9.99

☐ COLLECTED PLAYS: SIX (*The Good Person of Szechwan,*
   The Resistible Rise of Arturo Ui, Mr Puntila and his Man Matti)   £9.99

☐ COLLECTED PLAYS: SEVEN (*The Visions of Simone Machard,*
   Schweyk in the Second World War, The Caucasian Chalk Circle
   and Brecht's adaptation of *The Duchess of Malfi*)   £8.99

MODERN PLAYS

☐ CAUCASIAN CHALK CIRCLE   £6.99
☐ THE GOOD PERSON OF SZECHWAN   £7.99
☐ LIFE OF GALILEO   £6.99
☐ MOTHER COURAGE AND HER CHILDREN   £6.99
☐ THE RESISTIBLE RISE OF ARTURO UI   £6.99
☐ THE THREEPENNY OPERA   £6.99

● All Methuen Drama books are available through mail order or from your local bookshop.

Please send cheque/eurocheque/postal order (sterling only) Access, Visa, Mastercard, Diners Card, Switch or Amex.

Expiry Date:_____Signature: _____

Please allow 75 pence per book for post and packing U.K.
Overseas customers please allow £1.00 per copy for post and packing.

ALL ORDERS TO:

Methuen Books, Books by Post, TBS Limited, The Book Service, Colchester Road, Frating Green, Colchester, Essex CO7 7DW.

NAME: _____

ADDRESS: _____

_____

_____

Please allow 28 days for delivery. Please tick box if you do not
wish to receive any additional information   ☐

Prices and availability subject to change without notice.